Melchisedec

The Manifest

Sons of God!

Greg Crawford

Published by:

Creative Release Publishing

Des Moines, Iowa

thebaseiowa.org

Printed in the United States

First printing 2010

ISBN – 978-1481218870

Contents

Introduction

Introduction

We are at a seemingly critical moment in the divine time table of God. All are looking with anticipation for something to come but most do not know what they are really looking for. Some believe God will suddenly step in and do something sovereign. Others want another revival, but still others are happy with the status quo.

While we go through our spiritual hoops, the whole world is crying out for something real, something with substance. Many are dying going out into eternity; others struggle daily with demonic attacks which they don't even recognize. All the while the answer is sitting in the people of God.

We have preached to them with no results. What will it take to see men set free? Who will God call on in this hour the supposedly final hour of the Church? What kind of Christian will it take to rise up and begin to display heaven upon earth?

It will take manifest sons and daughters. Ones who operate as both king and priest. Ones who are in such relationship with the Father that their actions on the earth reflect His heart. Ones who walk in such authority that they manifest and display the heavenly realm upon the earth that they answer the cry of it and its inhabitants. Ones whose breath sets in motion the creative ability of God to change surroundings and answer the cry of all creation.

This short teaching book helps us understand the role of this new order of priests and their role in the earth. Written in more of an outline teaching notes, it will cause reasoning of what is being said, and also to be used as a teaching instruction resource. We need to be aware we could be one of those manifest sons or daughters destined to be raised up for such a time as this. It is my desire that we better understand the great depths of God and how His creative ability can flow through us as manifest sons and daughters.

Chapter 1

All Creation is Waiting

All creation is right now in a suspended place of anticipation for the manifestation of the sons of God. This anticipation is based on seeing the manifestation first of "The Son of God" and also previous "sons of God". We do not believe that what is not human could have anticipation. But in the multi-faceted dimensions of God, somehow all our actions come to bear on what God has created. After all, things in existence are sitting in an unredeemed state. The earth and all that is within it is suspended until the sons and daughters of God take their place and begin to speak with the very breath of God and begin to redeem all that is in the earth and bring it into submission to the Kingdom of God.

Romans 8:18-19 For I reckon that the sufferings of this present time are not worthy to be compared with the glory which shall be revealed in us. [19] For the earnest expectation of the creature waiteth for the manifestation of the sons of God.

Who are these sons of God and what is the manifestation that has such earnest expectation behind it? Many of us believe these sons of God are we, the believers. Others think it is some superstar evangelist. The above passage speaks of a glory that will be revealed. A Glory that, it appears, only these sons of God will be able to manifest. Even the wording is specific to a certain group.

2 Corinthians 3:9-10   For if the ministration of condemnation be glory, much more doth the ministration of righteousness exceed in glory . [10] For even that which was made glorious had no glory in this respect, by reason of the glory that excelleth.

The word 'glory' in these passages and in what the sons of God will manifest is both the same Greek meaning "Doxa". Doxa means a brightness and brilliance, reputation and fame. This glory is not the "Kabod" of God, or His presence, but is something that is beyond anointing. As we begin to look at this second passage in Corinthians, we see this same glory excelleth, or which means to throw beyond or to transcend. It appears what is to manifest is a type of Glory that is beyond what we have seen and also is transcended or transcended glory! This is the type of glory that we are changed from glory to glory. It is the resurrection glory that carries our spirit man from this dimension to another. This same glory is what God desires to be manifest upon these sons of God while upon the earth, not upon their death.

As we continue to read in Romans 8, we see that this type of glory also brings liberty and change that touches and effects all of us. We can all agree we have not yet seen the Church carrying such a glory. We have not seen the Church with brightness and brilliance, reputation and fame. But this manifestation will come as these sons of God are now being formed and starting to appear.

The word manifestation is what we are looking for. It comes from a Greek word meaning "metamorphous". It means to evolve. It is the same word as "transfiguration". It is about change that occurs inside that effect the outward appearance. So what are we looking for in this metamorphous, this transcended glory? Let's look again at our opening verse:

Romans 8:19 For the earnest expectation of the creature waiteth for the <u>manifestation</u> of the sons of God.

Manifestation in the Greek means "the appearing, the disclosure of truth and instruction, events by which things or states or persons hitherto withdrawn from view are made visible to all " So this manifestation is not some healing anointing or revivalist anointing but actually is about a truth carried so deeply in our spirits that it creates change within us. Then, as we allow it to take full form within us, it releases a transcended glory from us that is made visible to all around us!

2Corinthians 4:3-4 But if our gospel be hid, it is hid to them that are lost: [4] In whom the god of this world hath blinded the minds of them which believe not, lest the light of the glorious gospel of Christ, who is the image of God, should shine unto them.

This truth is not just knowledge but is something so deep that it lifts the veil of deception upon men's minds and they believe the Gospel! That is true illumination and brilliance. That is fame and reputation! That is the truth manifested!

Have there been manifest sons of God in the past? The answer is yes! The early Church had men like Paul who moved in this type of manifestation of truth that captivated the hearts of all those around them. We see men like Charles Parham who saw a truth of God concerning tongues and waited praying for that truth to manifest within him. The manifestation came, transcended glory was revealed and the earth's cry for the manifestation of the sons of God began to occur as thousands traveled into the mission field from the Azusa street outpouring. The result was the veil over the minds of men was lifted and they believed the Gospel. Others have followed in those steps. You see, it only takes a few carrying apostolic truth and allowing the transcended glory to manifest to begin to change the course of all things around.

Here are three simple things that make up a son of God:

1   First, you have those chosen of God to be pioneers in Truth in whatever stage of restoration.

2   Second, these chosen men are placed by God in a time and environment where their ministry comes to the front of all others in the world.

3   Ready for the challenge and prepared for the sacrifices. They anticipate the hate they must endure and face it with all joy.

4   They enter the process of allowing the truth to transcend their lives first and flow out of them to others second.

To be led by the Spirit of God!

Romans 8:14 For as many as are <u>led by the Spirit of God</u>, they are the sons of God.

The word 'led' is a word that means more than what we think of in definition of normal English language. Yes, it means to "lead" as in following someone or having followers. But it also means "to lead by laying hold of, and this way to bring to the point of destination, to lead by accompanying to (into) a place, attach to one's self as an attendant. "

It is allowing the Holy Spirit to have full control as we partner with Him. It is allowing God to lead us not in a one time event but into a process for our destiny to truly unfold. It is embracing what God has for us and not us deciding the direction or destiny our path will take. It is more than us saying, "wow! God used me in speaking a word, or the gifts, or witnessing!" It is so much more than that! It is completely wrapped up in a 24/7 awareness of the Spirit of God and the direction each moment is to take!

Purity and Christ likeness

1 John 3:1-3 Behold, what manner of love the Father hath bestowed upon us, that we should be called the sons of God: therefore the world knoweth us not, because it knew him not. [2] Beloved, now are we the sons of God, and <u>it doth not yet appear what we shall be</u>: but we know that, when he shall appear, we shall be like him; for we shall see him as he is . [3] And every man that hath this hope in him purifieth himself, even as he is pure.

God's outcome toward us is to call us sons because He loves us. This is one of the greatest honors we could have bestowed upon us. It is not anointings, or gifts of the Spirit, etc., but God's unconditional love that requires no performance. The statement is in verse 2 that "we are the sons of God". This is coming from us settling our identity issues and allowing the reflection of Christ to permeate our being. It then makes a statement that seems contrary to us being settled. It says "it does not yet appear what we shall be". The word 'appear' is the same word structure we see in Romans about the manifestation these sons of God will perform. The word 'appear' means "to make manifest, to make manifest or visible or known what has been hidden or unknown, be made known, expose to view, to become known, to be plainly recognized, thoroughly understood." You see, we have to be sons to allow the process and truth to be deposited within us. All of us are sons of God, but we are looking at a specific group of these sons, those who manifest a certain type of glory. That is why it states we do not know what is going to appear, because we are all in process. Some will fully manifest truth. Others may not. He gives the determining factor in verse 3. Purity is the separator that allows the process (hope) to manifest. The outcome is probably the grandest thing and confirms the full manifestation of the sons of God. It is in the definition above of manifest. As these sons of God appear, they will be seen, known, recognized and understood. That is bringing fame and reputation back to the Church!

Power to become Sons of God

John 1:12-13 But <u>as many as received him</u>, to them gave he power to become the sons of God, even to them that believe on his name : [13] Which were born, not of blood, nor of the will of the flesh, nor of the will of man, but of God.

The first step in the process of truly being a son of God is to receive Him. This is not a prayer of salvation. This is not even a decision to be open to all He would offer us. It means to take possession and ownership of Him! It is the right of inheritance.

The word 'receive' means to take with the hand, lay hold of, any person or thing in order to use it, to take in order to carry away, to make one's own, to associate with one's self as companion, to seize, apprehend. We see how Paul could say he was apprehended by God. It was not God taking hold of Paul but Paul saying he had firmly laid hold of Christ and had every intention of using what was available to him! It means that the power (right of inheritance) comes only after we have laid hold of Him in such a way that we are functioning in what has been given. This now puts us in the position of fulfilling destiny or the will (finished, no longer needing to exist) of God.

Shine as light because of the Word of God manifest

Philippians 2:14-16 Do all things without murmurings and disputings : 15 That ye may be blameless and harmless , the sons of God, without rebuke, in the midst of a crooked and perverse nation, among whom ye shine as lights in the world ; 16 Holding forth the word of life; that I may rejoice in the day of Christ, that I have not run in vain, neither laboured in vain .

What sets these sons of God apart is listed here in these verses. Notice it is not gifting or charisma, but is all about integrity and character. The sons of God are blameless, free from fault or defect. The sons of God are harmless, unmixed, pure as in wines or metals, without a mixture of evil, free from guile and innocent. The sons of God lead lives that require no rebuke, without reproach or in need of correction. The sons of God shine as light, illuminating in brightness and brilliance. The sons of God hold forth the Word of life and cherish it.

Romans 8:13-19 For if ye live after the flesh, ye shall die: but if ye through the Spirit do mortify the deeds of the body, ye shall live. 14 For as many as are led by the Spirit of God, they are the sons of God. 15 For ye have not received the spirit of bondage again to fear; but ye have received the Spirit of adoption, whereby we cry, Abba, Father. [16] The Spirit itself beareth witness with our spirit, that we are the children of God: [17] And if children, then heirs; heirs of God, and joint-heirs with Christ; if so be that we suffer with him, that we may be also glorified together. [18] For I reckon that the sufferings of this present time are not worthy to be compared with the glory which shall be revealed in us. [19] For the earnest expectation of the creature waiteth for the manifestation of the sons of God.

The only suffering the sons of God partake in the suffering is the moment of God of what God is birthing through them. But there is a glory that God desires to reveal through us and is made perfect in suffering. This glory is contrary to all things around, so we deny its manifestation. But these sons of God will be willing to lose reputation. They will hold and release revelation in new ways. They are already upon the earth and are being positioned to release new revelation and truth that will confront the religious structures men have built. When that happens, these sons of God will confront falseness because the manifestation of truth inside will be so great that it will demand a release to manifest and bring to bear all things!

As we continue on, we see that there is a Melchisedec Priesthood that is coming through these sons of God. **Hebrews 7** tells us that Jesus was a priest "in the order of Melchisedec". This means the priesthood He became a part of and functions as its high priest, was already in place. I will state that this priesthood is not the Old Testament priesthood. It is not the priesthood of Zadok and it is not the priesthood of the believers. It is a spiritual priesthood that Adam, Enoch, David and others functioned in.

Luke 24:32 And they said one to another, Did not our heart burn within us, while he talked with us by the way, and while he opened to us the scriptures?

These two men had walked with Jesus down the road for quite a while. But something was happening to them when they encountered the manifestation of truth that was occurring inside of Jesus. They were having an encounter with the Son of God, a Melchisedec priest operating! You see, when we encounter those who are allowing present or fresh truth from heaven to flow out of the depths of their spirit, that truth in them ignites the deposit of truth in us. This is how passions and zeal are birthed, by the ignition of truth. It is what we have been talking about in the past two teachings; transcended Glory, or that which brings change, illumination and fame of reputation!

This fire inside of them had no option but to be released and they brought it back to the other disciples, walking through the night, at risk to their own lives. True zeal and passion transcend human reasoning and excuses. It brings us to do things that are contrary to how we would normally respond or function.

Jeremiah 20:9 Then I said, I will not make mention of him, nor speak any more in his name. But his word was in mine heart as a burning fire shut up in my bones, and I was weary with forbearing, and I could not stay.

We read this passage concerning Jeremiah without a full understanding of what really has transpired. Prior to this, Jeremiah had decided he would not prophesy the word of the Lord. But then in this statement, he declares that it is like fire shut up in his bones. What he is talking about is the deposit that is inside of him could not be stopped and had to be released. It was not a past word or understanding that was creating the fire in his bones, but it was a current fresh word from God that was deposited inside and had to have expression. Once again, this is where that fiery passion and zeal comes from. A fresh word from God cannot be contained and will always have to be spoken and released if it truly is a fresh word from God. Jeremiah allowed the word of truth inside to be expressed again, releasing the fiery passion. He found out he could not contain this zeal! How different our prayer life, preaching and even conversations would be if we were all carrying a fresh word inside of us! Can you imagine the impact upon the earth that would be felt?

Isaiah 9:7 Of the increase of his government and peace there shall be no end, upon the throne of David, and upon his kingdom, to order it, and to establish it with judgment and with justice from henceforth even for ever. The zeal of the LORD of hosts will perform this.

There is something about God's zeal performing things and our zeal performing things. There is a huge difference. Zeal means "envious and jealousy". This zeal is referring to ownership. Zeal for another's property is envy. Zeal for your own property is jealousy. The zeal talked about here is that God has ownership of the property. WOW! I would not want to be in the way of God's zeal performing anything. You see, God's zeal is sovereign. It is connected to what He has decided to do and perform.

We see zeal listed in several places. We see that David had zeal for God's house in **Psalms 69:9**. David went on to say in **Psalms 119:139** that his zeal consumed him. David's zeal for the Lord was so consuming it became a channel to bring God to His people as a Melchisedec priest. David's jealousy for God so motivated him that it brought the people of God to God. This jealousy that David had was protective, to allow access to those truly seeking the Lord. His zeal was a motivation for people to bring a desire for God that they did not have. Jealousy really is restrained desire. It is where we birth and maintain our anticipation and expectations. Zeal is really restrained passions. It is where we birth and maintain intimacy and our relationship with the Lord. God has both jealousy and zeal towards us, but most of the time it is restrained. If He would fully express both of these to us, we would not be able to contain such overwhelming love in these physical bodies. Jealousy defies natural law. It is what allows us to gain access into third heaven. It is where we see the ownership of God and His blessings. Zeal is what releases the third heaven into the earth realm. It is what touches the physical realm with the heavenly. It is what brings the reality of what we are passionate about (hidden motive) to be seen or expressed outwardly. When we get this kind of fresh word inside us concerning present truth into situations, then we will see the Kingdom come in far greater dynamics than what we have seen in past times. This is what all creation is waiting for, the grandest display of manifestation that has ever occurred!

Colossians 4:12-13 Epaphras, who is one of you, a servant of Christ, saluteth you, always labouring fervently for you in prayers, that ye may stand perfect and complete in all the will of God. 13 For I bear him record, that he hath a great zeal for you, and them that are in Laodicea, and them in Hierapolis.

Epaphras had not only zeal but a great zeal. It was something that excelled and made him atypical. It set him apart in such a way that Paul had to mention his name. This word 'zeal' here means: "fervor, to boil with heat, a state of passionate commitment'! Webster's defines zeal as "eager interest and pursuit of something". Epaphras was pursuing alright. Pursuing not his interests but the interest of others. His zeal was to see Christ formed in others. His interest was not for just a couple of people but all those in three major cities.

I like the definition of a passionate commitment. I believe most of us have seen the commitment levels so low in projects or undertakings we have done. I believe the problem is we are trying to do these things on our own human zeal and not letting the zeal of the Lord consume us with what He is zealous for. True zeal comes from the Holy Spirit. **Rom 12:11** says fervent in Spirit, serving the Lord. This is not so much the human spirit but the Spirit of God inside of us. When we allow the Spirit of God to show us or deposit a fresh word in us, jealousy or ownership of that word will be expressed in passion, or what we waste our time and resources on. This is what the world is looking for and the Lord is longing for. Then the world will desire what the Church has. We will go out and turn the world upside down. We will impact nations, confront demonic forces and see impact as we become the manifestation of the sons of God!

Chapter 2

The foundations of Priesthood
Two Priesthoods Revealed

There are two priesthood models found in the Bible, Aaron's and Melchisedec. So that we do not confuse the two, we will first look briefly into Aaron's and then into the order of Melchisedec. First, let me say we are doing this because the priesthood of Aaron is not the priesthood of Melchisedec. The Order of Melchisedec is a higher level than that of Aaron's.

Aaron's priesthood came from the disciplines of God's ways. It was run by a Levitical priest who had determined priesthood based on lineage. This priesthood tried to reflect holiness unto the Lord without really carrying the nature of the Lord. It was a priesthood whose sole focus was ministry to the Lord through natural sacrifices.

In comparison, the Priesthood of Melchisedec was a spiritual priesthood not chosen by lineage but by intimacy and a heart towards God. It was a priesthood walking in full redemption because of internal consecration which released authority. This allowed the very nature of God to be seen in them, allowing them access to minister to both God and the people of God.

Aaron's Priesthood was first seen in *Ex. 28:1-40.* There is fire on the mountain, angelic hosts are present, the priestly garments are made and the priesthood is installed. Priests were installed as they were set in place by blood and anointing oil upon their lives. They were dedicated to the Lord by the killing of a young bullock on the altar. Here are the simple steps Aaron took as a priest to be installed.

Lev. 8:1-30

Step 1   Aaron was brought to the altar – marriage of him to the nation and the nation to the Lord.

Step 2   Aaron washed with water – separation

Step 3   Clothed with the garment of a high priest

Step 4   Anointed with oil

Step 5   Sacrifices were made to consecrate the priest into function

Step 6   A ram was killed and its blood anointed the right ear, right thumb, right toe. This symbolized his prophetic hearing, working, and walk.

Step 7   Oil and blood was mixed and put upon the priest's garments symbolizing his complete surrender of his life for the life God had for him as a priest.

The main role of Aaron's priesthood was to make sacrifices for the people as the mediator between God and them. But what was lacking was intimacy with the Lord. They had encounters with God and could hear the voice of the Lord. They saw the hand of God, but for the most part they lacked true intimacy. Over the years, they did the function of anointed priest but it became so common that the encounters with God disappeared, the hand of God was not seen, and the voice of God was not heard. **Heb. 9-11** says this first covenant ---- this action of bulls and calves and blood could not purify the individual people. The priests were operating for the sake of an entire nation not as individuals. In other words, the priest could not bring holiness to the people by their actions.

So God sent an unnamed man of God to confront Eli the current priest. Eli had been violating the functions of priest and so had his sons.

1 Samuel 2:27-34 And there came a man of God unto Eli, and said unto him, Thus saith the LORD, Did I plainly appear unto the house of thy father, when they were in Egypt in Pharaoh's house ? [28] And did I choose him out of all the tribes of Israel to be my priest, to offer upon mine altar, to burn incense, to wear an ephod before me? and did I give unto the house of thy father all the offerings made by fire of the children of Israel ? [29] Wherefore kick ye at my sacrifice and at mine offering, which I have commanded in my habitation; and <u>honourest thy sons above me</u>, to <u>make yourselves fat with the chiefest of all the offerings of Israel my people</u> ? [30] Wherefore the LORD God of Israel saith, <u>I said indeed that thy house, and the house of thy father, should walk before me for ever:</u> but now the LORD saith, Be it far from me; for them that honour me I will honour, and they that despise me shall be lightly esteemed . [31] Behold, the days come, that I will cut off thine arm, and the arm of thy father's house, that there shall not be an old man in thine house . [32] And thou shalt see an enemy in my habitation, in all the wealth which God shall give Israel: and there shall not be an old man in thine house for ever . [33] And the man of thine, whom I shall not cut off from mine altar, shall be to consume thine eyes, and to grieve thine heart: and all the increase of thine house shall die in the *flower of their age . ³⁴ And this shall be a sign unto thee, that shall come upon thy two sons, on Hophni and Phinehas; in one day they shall die both of them.*

Eli had violated the conditions of the existence of the priesthood and made it of no effect for the people. He was the fulfillment of an earlier prophecy that the priesthood was taken from Abiathar, descendant of Aaron's son Ithamar, and given to Zadok, descendant of Aaron's son, Eleazar in **1 Kings 2:27, 35** . God was changing the lineage to begin to purify the priesthood again.

Numbers 3:4 And Nadab and Abihu died before the LORD, when they offered strange fire before the LORD, in the wilderness of Sinai, and they had no children: and Eleazar and Ithamar ministered in the priest's office in the sight of Aaron their father .

By the withdrawal of the high priesthood from Eleazar, the elder of Aaron's two sons (after Nadab and Abihu were destroyed, (**Num 3:4**), that dignity had been conferred on the family of Ithamar, to which Eli belonged, and now that his descendants had forfeited the honor, it was to be taken from them and restored to the elder branch. This was about restoration and setting the priesthood back into order.

1 Samuel 2:35-36 <u>And I will raise me up a faithful priest, that shall do according to that which is in</u>

mine heart and in my mind: and I will build him a
sure house; and he shall walk before mine anointed
for ever . [36] *And it shall come to pass, that every*
one that is left in thine house shall come and
crouch to him for a piece of silver and a morsel of
bread, and shall say, Put me, I pray thee, into one
of the priests' offices, that I may eat a piece of
bread .

Prophetically it is speaking of David as a type of
Melchisedec priest and of Jesus the "High priest of
our profession" *Heb. 3:1.* David is called a priest
forever after the order of Melchisedec in **Ps. 110**.
David was not a priest in the Levitical order nor in
the order of Aaron's lineage. David did take the
ephod, a priestly act, in **1 Sam. 30** and bound from
the Lord to 'pursue and recover all'. He was
operating not as a Levitical priest but as a
Melchisedec priest/king.

Melchisedec priests allow the house of the
Lord to be built. David allowed this and so did
Jesus. *Heb. 3:2 -6 "whose house are we".* Looking at
some definitions in *1 Sam. 2:35-36,* gives us more
insights. (KJV)

[35] *And I will raise me up a faithful priest, that shall*
do according to that which is in mine heart and in my
mind: and I will build him a sure house; and he shall
walk before mine anointed for ever. [36] *And it shall*

come to pass, that every one that is left in thine house shall come and crouch to him for a piece of silver and a morsel of bread, and shall say, Put[g] me, I pray thee, into one of the priests' offices, that I may eat a piece of bread.

Do = to execute, to work, produce and fashion, to act with an effect, to put in order (reformation)

According to = thinking, reflection, memory. *1A5* inclination, resolution, determination (of will). *1A6* conscience. *1A7* heart (of moral character). *1A8* as seat of appetites. *1A9* as seat of emotions and passions.

Heart = same as according to

Mind = the breath coming from the very existence of the being, the activity of character

Before = in front of or out in front

By looking at these definitions, we see that both David and Jesus fulfilled this! The shifting in priesthood to Zadok did not accomplish these definitions!

We know that just as was said, Eli's sons are dead and Eli falls dead as well, now there is no more lineage of priesthood from this family! So God always has provision (not a backup plan) and there remains a priest but not a high priest or sons to assume the role of high priest. Under Aaron's other two sons is a lineage of priests as well. Eleazar, from which Zadok descends and Ithamar, from which Abithar descends.

Samuel anoints David as king and Saul begins a conflict with him. During this time, Saul kills most of the priests and Abiathar flees to the cave of Adullam to be with David. *1 Sam. 22:20.*

Zadok remains with Saul as his priest, until Saul is killed. Now David has a priest as well, which enables him to be able to carry the ark back in later. At this point, there are two distinct priests operating under two different type of leaders.

Finally, David takes the throne and all functioning priests come under his authority. The problem is that he has two functioning high priests, Abiathar and Zadok. Both are from the lineage of Aaron and both are functioning. So David appoints both to function at the same time to avoid violating Levitical law by removing a high priest from functioning without a reason. Zadok, under the Tabernacle of Moses pattern and Abiathar, under David's new Tabernacle pattern. One with the ark and one without. The priesthood now goes through a transition but not a change of function!

1 Chronicles 16:38-41 And Obededom with their brethren, threescore and eight; Obededom also the son of Jeduthun and Hosah to be porters : <u>*39 And Zadok the priest, and his brethren the priests, before the tabernacle of the LORD in the high place that was at Gibeon ,*</u> <u>*40 To offer burnt offerings unto the LORD upon the altar of the burnt offering continually morning and evening, and to do according to all that is written in the law of the LORD, which he commanded Israel ;*</u> *41 And with them Heman and Jeduthun, and the rest that were chosen, who were expressed by name, to give thanks to the LORD, because his mercy endureth for ever ;*

It comes under the influence of Melchisedec's priest, David. It is a governing priesthood based in intimacy. David's intimacy dictates the function of the temple but the priesthood natural function remains the same. Zadok is still functioning under Levitical priesthood while the new is operating! We learn later that David does this because the sons of Zadok held fast to holiness. This is the bare minimum standard of all priests and the expectation of God has not only returned but held over years. This holding fast was because of being under the influence of governing by intimacy.

Zadok is not a new order of priesthood but the reordering of it back to the original intention.

He is not Melchisedec but is a type of the priesthood of all believers.

Eventually Abiathar is part of the rebellion and he loses his position as high priest. Zadok is installed under David's influence as God appointed Zadok as well to come under the influence of David's new pattern to infuse new life into an old priesthood. Because David acted as a Melchizedek Priest, something happens to the priesthood, it is restored to what it was to be and intended to be. It reached the point that the Sons of Zadok held fast for years and later were the only ones found worthy to be involved in constructing the temple anew. Solomon takes over from David and appoints Zadok as high priest as well.

Zadok and the Zadokites grow in strength, power and influence over the years. Then captivity occurs and Solomon's temple is destroyed. It is rebuilt as Ezekiel says, by the Sons of Zadok. To maintain control and because of the influences they had, they adopted what is called sadduceeism doctrine.

Zadok's priesthood lineage finally became corrupted again and eventual ends up as the Sadducees priest who take their name TSDOKI from the name TSADOK which is Zadok and try to take that role as priest. God still needs a new order of priest, uncompromising, birthed in intimacy, both as kings and priest.

Greg Crawford

Chapter 3

The Spirit Within

There are three distinct levels of spiritual release in scripture

Ministering from Anointing
Ministering when the Spirit comes upon
Ministering from the nature of God resident within

Anointing

Anoint means "to rub upon, to smear with oil, pour upon, assignment". Anointing is the divine enablement of God to do something spiritual through imperfect vessels. In the Old Testament, anointing was symbolic of being set part as holy. It meant divine favor and was a sign of it upon your life. It did not mean your character was fully developed, but that God had chosen you as a vessel for His use. Anointing does not make you holy it only signifies you yield to the Spirit to work through you to others. The **1 Cor. 12** gifts are anointing not nature.

Anointing is part of the equipping for service (present tense - not completed). Anointing has the option of the person both receiving and accepting what is being given.

Spirit Upon

Numbers 11:25[5] And the LORD came down in a cloud, and spake unto him, and took of the spirit that was upon him, and gave it unto the seventy elders: and it came to pass, that , when the spirit rested upon them, they prophesied, and did not cease

Numbers 24:2-6 And Balaam lifted up his eyes, and he saw Israel abiding in his tents according to their tribes; and the spirit of God came upon him. [3] And he took up his parable, and said, Balaam the son of Beor hath said, and the man whose eyes are open hath said : [4] He hath said, which heard the words of God, which saw the vision of the Almighty, falling into a trance , but having his eyes open : [5] How goodly are thy tents, O Jacob, and thy tabernacles, O Israel ! [6] As the valleys are they spread forth, as gardens by the river's side, as the trees of lign aloes which the LORD hath planted, and as cedar trees beside the waters .

Judges 3:9-10 And when the children of Israel cried unto the LORD, the LORD raised up a deliverer to the children of Israel, who delivered them, even Othniel the son of Kenaz, Caleb's younger brother . [10] And the Spirit of the LORD came upon him, and he judged Israel, and went out to war: and the LORD delivered Chushanrishathaim king of Mesopotamia into his hand; and his hand prevailed against Chushanrishathaim .

Judges 6:34 But the Spirit of the LORD came upon Gideon, and he blew a trumpet; and Abiezer was gathered after him.

1 Samuel 10:9-10 And it was so , that when he had turned his back to go from Samuel, God gave him another heart: and all those signs came to pass that day . ¹⁰ And when they came thither to the hill, behold, a company of prophets met him; and the Spirit of God came upon him, and he prophesied among them.

1 Samuel 16:13 Then Samuel took the horn of oil, and anointed him in the midst of his brethren: and the Spirit of the LORD came upon David from that day forward. So Samuel rose up, and went to Ramah .

In all of these examples, we see the Spirit upon them for a one time event giving extraordinary power and ability. When David was anointed by Samuel, what also happened was the Spirit came upon him. Something unique happened with David that showed a greater sign of God's approval. The Spirit came upon him from that day forward. This actually means the ability for the Spirit to come upon was there and the Spirit came upon him readily and many times. It was a stating of an opening David had privilege to. The Spirit resting upon a person causes a sanctification process and enabled David as a king for him to qualify him for priesthood.

Spirit Within

The Spirit within us is the nature of God enabling the heart of God to come with His words and breath behind them. It is a deposit that is living and alive within us. When the Spirit is within, it gives no option but removes excuses and creates.

1 Samuel 2:35 And I will raise me up a faithful priest, that shall do according to that which is in mine heart and in my mind: and I will build him a sure house; and he shall walk before mine anointed for ever .

David was spoken of being a faithful priest both knowing the heart of God and doing it upon the earth. Notice it states in this role he will be distinguished from those anointed. It is at a higher level. It is an ongoing walk, or display of life for all to see.

Spirit Within Melchisedec Priesthood

Luke 4:18-19 The Spirit of the Lord is upon me, because he hath anointed me to preach the gospel to the poor; he hath sent me to heal the brokenhearted, to preach deliverance to the captives, and recovering of sight to the blind, to set at liberty them that are bruised , ¹⁹ To preach the acceptable year of the Lord .

Anointed means "assigned, consecration, to function in an Messianic office"

Here Jesus says

1. The spirit is upon me – ready for a one time event
2. I am anointed
3. I am sent --- the nature of God sent

Jesus was sent not as a man but as a reflection of the Father. He reflected His character, His nature and His breath forming His Father's wishes upon the earth. Jesus ministered from the nature within Him that had no limitation!

John 3:34 For he whom God hath sent speaketh the words of God: for God giveth not the Spirit by measure unto him .

The key to His success in ministry was that He only did what He saw His father do, He said what

His father said and created what His father desired. Jesus spoke and carried the breath of life within His words. This always created life from the nature of God within Him. This always brought authority over any situation. This always ministered to God and to people simultaneously!

Romans 8:10-19 And if Christ be in you, the body is dead because of sin; but the Spirit is life because of righteousness . [11] But if the Spirit of him that raised up Jesus from the dead dwell in you, he that raised up Christ from the dead shall also <u>quicken</u> your mortal bodies by his Spirit that <u>dwelleth</u> in you .

quicken means to produce life or cause to live, new and greater powers of life, to increase life itself --- to make alive

Dwelleth means a fixed position of influencing as dwells means to only inhabit but may not have action with it.

[12] Therefore, brethren, we are debtors, not to the flesh, to live after the flesh . [13] For if ye live after the flesh, ye shall die: but if ye through the Spirit do mortify the deeds of the body, ye shall live . [14] For as many as are led by the Spirit of God, they are the sons of God .

Led means "to lay hold of, to be accompanied, forces and influences of the mind".

[15] For ye have not received the spirit of bondage again to fear; but ye have received the Spirit of

adoption, whereby we cry, Abba, Father . [16] The Spirit itself beareth witness with our spirit, that we are the children of God :

[17] And if children, then heirs; heirs of God, and joint-heirs with Christ; if so be that we suffer with him , that we may be also glorified together . [18] For I reckon that the sufferings of this present time are not worthy to be compared with the glory which shall be revealed in us . [19] For the earnest expectation of the creature waiteth for the manifestation of the sons of God .

revealed means "to uncover, lay open what has been veiled or covered up. 1A disclose, make bare"

manifestation means "coming" once, and "appearing" once. **1** a laying bare, making naked. **2** a disclosure of truth, instruction. 2A concerning things before unknown.

What all creation is longing for is the manifestation of all three dynamics of the Spirit at once, anointing, the Spirit upon and the Spirit within. In other words, those who have allowed the Spirit to fully consume them to become vessels the Father can flow through unrestricted!

Greg Crawford

Chapter 4

Jesus is a Melchisedec Priest

There are two priesthood models in the Bible, Aaron's and Melchisedec. Aaron's priesthood came from the disciplines of God while Melchisedec comes from the intentions of God's heart. The difference can be seen with some study and insights. The main distinguishing mark of the Melchisedec priesthood is the sacrifice of this priesthood offered will be their very lives as they position themselves into the heart of God to be able to minister to the people of God.

There is much debate concerning where did the Melchisedec priesthood originate. There is no real focus upon it but yet it seems to always exist. The scriptures allude to Jesus not starting this priesthood but coming into the order of it. This dispels that Jesus started it while here on the earth. Let's look at the scriptures and see what insights can be gained.

Genesis 14:16-20 And he brought back all the goods, and also brought again his brother Lot, and his goods, and the women also, and the people . 17 And the king of Sodom went out to meet him after his return from the slaughter of Chedorlaomer, and of the kings that were with him, at the valley of

Shaveh, which is the king's dale . [18] <u>And</u>
<u>Melchizedek king of Salem brought forth bread and</u>
<u>wine: and he was the priest of the most high God .</u>
[19] And he blessed him, and said, Blessed be Abram
of the most high God, possessor of heaven and
earth : [20] And blessed be the most high God, which
hath delivered thine enemies into thy hand. And he
gave him tithes of all.

Noah had a son, Shem, who was the king of
Salem. Shem lived life in the Spirit and built the
city of Salem, which means peace, a city of
righteousness. As both a king and priest, he
brought bread and wine, which represents the
power to bless with provision and that which
sustains. He had the power to release God's
blessing upon Abraham in such a way that
Abraham recognized it and desired this blessing. It
appears Abraham had no problem tithing to
Melchisedec as well. Tithing was only done
upward and to those recognized as having greater
spiritual authority over you. Since at this time,
Abraham had not yet become the father of many
nations, or the father of righteousness, an
interesting thing is seen here. Abraham was
probably being heavily influenced by both the King
of Salem, Melchisedec, and the city he had built-
Salem, city of righteousness. We can only assume
the Kingly/Priestly influence of righteousness just

did not appear but was cultivated by this influence to enable God to declare he would be the father of this righteousness in the earth.

Now what is important to note is that Melchizedek means not a title but a function. "**Melchisedec**" was never meant to be a name. The Hebrew 'melek' means king and 'tsedeq' means righteousness. It means "*my king is Sedek*". *Sedek means "the rightful shoot" or "King of Righteousness".*
"

You see, Abraham was destined to be the father of righteousness but Melchisedec was the king of righteousness. One was a propagator of righteousness and the other was the governing oversight of righteousness!

Hebrews 5:1-9 (KJV)
[1] For every high priest taken from among men is ordained for men in things pertaining to God, that he may offer both gifts and sacrifices for sins: [2] Who can have compassion on the ignorant, and on them that are out of the way; for that he himself also is compassed with infirmity. [3] And by reason hereof he ought, as for the people, so also for himself, to offer for sins. [4] And no man taketh this honour unto himself, but he that is called of God, as was Aaron. [5] So also Christ glorified not himself

to be made an high priest; but he that said unto him, Thou art my Son, to day have I begotten thee. [6] As he saith also in another place, Thou art a priest for ever after the order of Melchisedec. [7] Who in the days of his flesh, when he had offered up prayers and supplications with strong crying and tears unto him that was able to save him from death, and was heard in that he feared; [8] Though he were a Son, yet learned he obedience by the things which he suffered; [9] And being made perfect, he became the author of eternal salvation unto all them that obey him;

This is the priesthood ordained for men. Vs.1 Ordained for men. This is a priesthood that must suffer for the ministry's sake and not suffer because of ministry opportunity. It is a suffering because of what you are doing, not because of life circumstances. It is only associated with your actions for Christ, and you knowingly implementing them that you will enter into suffering. It refers to actions that causes us great discomfort but also produces positive results, so we freely enter the suffering.

Hebrews 5:10 Called of God an high priest after the order of Melchisedec.

Hebrews 6:20 Whither the forerunner is for us entered, even Jesus, made an high priest for ever after the order of Melchisedec.

In these verses, he is saying that Jesus was after the order of and not the start of this priesthood. Meaning the priesthood was already established. This priesthood was unique in the fact it was a forerunner of those who entered the revelatory realm through the way provided.

Hebrews 7:1-2 For this Melchisedec, king of Salem, priest of the most high God, who met Abraham returning from the slaughter of the kings, and blessed him; [2] To whom also Abraham gave a tenth part of all; first being by interpretation King of righteousness, and after that also King of Salem, which is, King of peace;

This priesthood was always in the heart of God. It had no beginning or ending, in other words, it is an eternal priesthood, unlike Aaron's being temporal while the person is on the earth. These Melchisedec priests are priest forever and throughout eternity. Having no mother or father, it is a spiritual priesthood not born into like Aaron's, having descendents.

Hebrews 7:3 Without father, without mother, without descent , having neither beginning of days, nor end of life; <u>but made like unto the Son of God</u>; abideth a priest continually .

What is meant by "without father, without mother, without descent, having neither beginning of days or end of life"? The phrase "without descent" is translated from the Greek *agenealogetos*. This word does not mean the absence of ancestors, but the absence of a traced genealogy. To the Jews, a traceable genealogy was of utmost importance, especially for the priesthood. If one could not prove his lineage, he was barred from being a priest (**Nehemiah 7:64**). There is no recorded genealogy of Melchisedec. His descent was not important because his priesthood was not dependant on it. His lineage did not affect his right to the priesthood.

The Aaronic priests could not begin to serve as a priest until they were twenty-five years old, and had to retire when they reached the age of fifty (**Numbers 4:1-3, 22-23, 35, 43; 8:24-25**). Age was very important to the Aaronic priesthood, but not to Melchisedec's.

These priests resemble Christ. They are made into the exact image of Him with similar traits, character, functions, and motives of heart. They carry the very breath of God within them.

Made like means to cause a model to pass off into an image or shape like it. **2** to express itself in it, to copy. **3** to produce a facsimile. **4** to be made like, render similar. Coming from a root word meaning a separation or breaking <u>a union with something in</u> <u>fellowship with</u> <u>the origin of the cause</u>

Hebrews 7:10-11 For he was yet in the loins of his father, when Melchisedec met him. If therefore perfection were by the Levitical priesthood, (for under it the people received the law,) what further need was there that another priest should rise after the order of Melchisedec, and not be called after the order of Aaron?

Our current understanding of priesthood is under the order of Aaron , ones who do service unto God. The Priesthood coming is under the order of Melchisedec. Our service unto God is to carry and display His Glory to others upon the earth.

Hebrews 7:15 And it is yet far more evident: for that after the similitude of Melchisedec there ariseth another priest,

Here the words, "After the *similitude* of Melchisedec there ariseth *another* priest." The Greek word translated "similitude" is *homoioteta* which indicates "that Jesus is *similar to*, but not the *same as*, Melchisedec. Jesus' priesthood is being compared to, or likened to Melchisedec's priesthood. The author did not say that Jesus is Melchisedec or vice versa, but rather that Jesus has a priesthood similar to Melchisedec's.

Hebrews 7:17 For he testifieth, Thou art a priest for ever after the order of Melchisedec.

Notice again that Jesus is not identified as being Melchisedec, but is identified as having a priesthood after *his* order. This implies that Melchisedec and Jesus were two different individuals. One cannot compare one's priesthood to another's if they are already the same thing. Likewise, the author of Hebrews could not compare the order of Jesus' priesthood to Melchisedec's if Melchisedec was Jesus. If Melchisedec was Jesus, He would not have a priesthood to compare His own to, because He already possessed the only eternal priesthood that existed. If only one person has only one thing, then a comparison cannot be made. Comparisons can only be made between two or more related persons or things.

Hebrews 7:21 (For those priests were made without an oath; but this with an oath by him that said unto him, The Lord sware and will not repent, Thou art a priest for ever after the order of Melchisedec:)

(From Charles Price Prophecy) (quote)

"*Some trials will be absolute necessity for clearing away the remaining infirmity of the natural mind and burning of all wood, nothing shall remain in the fire, for as the refiner's fire, so shall he purify the sons of the kingdom.*"

"*Some will be fully redeemed, being clothed upon with a priestly garment after Melchisedec order, qualifying them for governing authority; for it is required on their part to suffer the fanning of the fiery breath, searching every part within them until they arrive at a fixed body from whence the wonders is to flow. Upon this body will be the fixation of the Urim and Thumim that are the portion of the Melchisedec priesthood, whose genealogy is not counted in the creation which is under the fall, but in another genealogy which is the new creation. These priests will have a deep inward search and divine sights into secret things of deity. They will be able to prophesy on clear grounds, not darkly or enigmatically, for they will know what is couched in the first originality of all beings, in the eternal antitype of nature, and will be able to bring them forth according to divine counsel and ordination. The Lord sweareth in truth and righteousness that from Abraham's seed after the spirit, there shall arise a holy seed which shall be manifested in the last age.*" (end quote)

Priests speak to God for the people; Prophets speak to the people for God. A king is a leader of the people, which sometimes will represent the whole people. But the reason why we need a priesthood or a prophet line is because God prefers to deal directly with individual people rather than having the king to represent all of them. The priest cannot only bring the sacrifice of the king before God, but he can also bring the sacrifice of anybody from among the people before God. The priest speaks to God for the people, while the prophet is the mouthpiece of God to the people. In the end of days when there shall be the new heavens and the new earth, these priests of the order of Melchisedec will still be ministering to God. They have to be of unchangeable priesthood to be priests perhaps for the whole physical universe. Christ is uniting all things in heaven and in earth into Himself.

"For it pleased the Father that in him should all fulness dwell; And having made peace through the blood of his cross, by him to reconcile all things unto himself; by him, I say, whether they be things in earth, or things in heaven". (Col.1:19-20).

The power of the Melchisedec Priesthood is to administer the ordinances of the Gospel with divine authority; and to have those ordinances recorded in heaven. This comes because of the inward dwelling of Christ with the ability to set things in order. As priest of the Lord, they are aligning earth to the intentions of His heart with great power and authority.   This emerging order or company will have the Shekinah Glory not upon them but within them. They minister out of a deep place that is beyond anointing. It literally is the fullness of the deposit with them that is ministering.   The best way to describe what I have now come to say is a "Melchisedec Word" is to give a couple of examples. Before I do, I will say this, I do not minister like this as much as I would like and these words come as we connect ourselves in a greater fashion than recognizing and yielding to the anointing. I would say this depth comes seldom, but when it comes, the results are staggering.

The first time I released a word of this magnitude, I was so deep in the spirit I was almost caught away. I was in Oberlin, Ohio ministering at a conference. I released a prophetic word that carried so much weight it literally knocked every person to the ground. No one moved and the meeting was concluded as no one could speak. This was a meeting made up of almost all five fold ministers used to strong anointing. My wife said you literally could not stand under the weight of it.

A second time, I was at a conference and the Lord said I would only speak 5 words and He would invade. The words were "tonight your innocence is restored". Every person in the room hit the floor in deep tears as wailing broke forth and healing occurred. I have given these types of words since then and I must admit the outcome is far greater than any anointing I have ever witnessed.

One way I describe this is it is the third dimension of Glory. What do I mean? It looks like this:

Mankind --- application of glory
Jesus – reflection of Glory
Father – essence of glory

It is not just application or reflection but it is the release of the very essence of the Father that carries within it the creative ability to put things n motion that have not been. It is coming out of being a mature son or daughter.

Ephesians 4:13 Till we all come in the unity of the faith, and of the knowledge of the Son of God, unto a perfect man, unto the measure of the stature of the fulness of Christ :

Chapter 5

The functioning Priesthood Coming

Psalm 110 The LORD said unto my Lord, Sit thou at my right hand, until I make thine enemies thy footstool . ² The LORD shall send the rod of thy strength out of Zion: rule thou in the midst of thine enemies . ³ Thy people shall be willing in the day of thy power, in the beauties of holiness from the womb of the morning: thou hast the dew of thy youth . ⁴ <u>The LORD hath sworn, and will not repent, Thou art a priest for ever after the order of Melchizedek</u>. ⁵ The Lord at thy right hand shall strike through kings in the day of his wrath . ⁶ He shall judge among the heathen, he shall fill the places with the dead bodies; he shall wound the heads over many countries . ⁷ He shall drink of the brook in the way: therefore shall he lift up the head .

      This Melchisedec priesthood will carry with it a Jubilee anointing of freedom and liberty. *Lev. 25, Is. 61, Luke 4:18*. After all, Jesus shifted from a day of vengeance to a day of favor when he quoted *Isaiah 61*. It will be a total freedom brought by the Glory of God and not by the convincing of men's words.

1 Samuel 2:32-35 [2] *And thou shalt see an enemy in my habitation, in all the wealth which God shall give Israel: and there shall not be an old man in thine house for ever .* [33] *And the man of thine, whom I shall not cut off from mine altar, shall be to consume thine eyes, and to grieve thine heart: and all the increase of thine house shall die in the flower of their age .* [34] *And this shall be a sign unto thee, that shall come upon thy two sons, on Hophni and Phinehas; in one day they shall die both of them.* [35] *And I will raise me up a faithful priest, <u>that shall do according to that which is in mine heart and in my mind:</u> and I will build him a sure house; and he shall walk before mine anointed for ever .*

We see that David was a Melchisedec priest who brought the Glory of God to a nation and eventually the world would come to see its display through his son, Solomon. The standard is seen in the above verse, doing the heart of God!

Do means to execute, to work, produce and fashion, to act with an effect, to put in order (reformation)

According to means thinking, reflection, memory. *1A5* inclination, resolution, determination (of will). *1A6* conscience. *1A7* heart (of moral character). *1A8* as seat of appetites. *1A9* as seat of emotions and passions.

Heart means same as according to

Mind means the breath coming from the very existence of the being, the activity of character

Before means in front of or out in front

He will establish this priest as a dwelling or habitation and he will walk BEFORE my anointed. In other words, at a higher place. This priesthood will be beyond the anointing, but carry the very breath of God. Ministering with His words with the very breath infusing His character and presence into the situation.

For David to have God's heart, he had five distinct things.

1.David's <u>love for the Lord</u> was all-consuming and allowed the desire of God to be brought to his people.

2. David's <u>desire of the people</u> motivated him to establish a means for them to have intimacy with God.

3. David <u>acted as a king</u> carrying the government of God

4.David was <u>called as a warrior</u> to defend the Kingdom of God.

5.David <u>unified the people</u> of God into the spiritual force.

David was beginning to move in the next age and was beginning to model an age that was coming. David was the type and shadow of the Melchisedec priesthood which is governing by intimacy. Intimacy without governing is not Kingdom and is not Melchisedec as well. True Melchisedec priests will also begin to manifest the fullness of redemption and not just a small portion.

Melchisedec priests will usher in the next Millennium

- They will be participators of the Kingdom age.
- They will be anticipators of the eternal age.
- They will be fully functioning in the present age.

Chapter 6

Melchisedec Restoring Innocence

This Priesthood is marked by unprecedented Holiness --- the same as Christ Himself. "Be ye holy like I am holy" is not an invitation but a command. "Holiness unto the Lord" is not an action but a people. Holiness will not be a result of encounters, but will be a lifestyle that will begin to bring encounters forth. This priest will bring forth the breath of God from God's heart right into situations.

Part of what this priesthood will do is the restoration of innocence. They will be carriers of this innocence enabling them to have great power over any situation they are in. Webster defines innocence as 'a freedom from guilt or sin through being unacquainted with evil, lack of worldly experience or sophistication, lack of knowledge'. Biblical innocence is defined as 'to be free from guilt, to be pure, TO BE FREE FROM OBLIGATION, harmless in intention, free from legal guilt'.

Many have had their innocence stolen from them. Riddled with guilt and hopelessness, many Christians are no different than those not born again. Lost innocence can also mean we have experienced things that might have tainted us as well. This keeps us far from God out of shame and guilt. The reason of this restoration of innocence is all intimacy requires innocence. God will restore innocence to many so intimacy will deepen.

Genesis 2:7⁷ And the LORD God formed man of the dust of the ground, and breathed into his nostrils the breath of life; and man became a living soul .

God breathed means to blow, cause to blow or to actually loose life!

God breathed life into Adam and Eve, He did not breathe life into the animals. The breath or life God breathed into Adam had His nature in it. When Adam fell, he lost innocence by tainting the nature of God within him. Innocence is taken when we take from the wrong tree.

Adam was destined to live in two things, pure Holiness and full Righteousness. **Innocence is the original form of righteousness and the purest form of holiness.** But sin made us unrighteous and stole and continues to steal innocence. What the devil stole was not Adam and Eve's life but he tried take the Breath. The Breath of God that had innocence attached to it._ God created things in innocence. When the Spirit hovered over the deep, it was a deliberate act of waiting. Waiting for the breath to come with the word – to create, perform, and release the path. What God creates is always created in an innocent state. What we see in the spirit realm from heaven is generally in this state as well. We see a vision for our lives in the purest state. When it comes to earth, we then see it through sin trying to taint it. We lose heart because it appears to not be in the original state. It is the same, the devil is trying to steal both the vision and destiny and the innocence it had as well.

Genesis 3:8 the Voice or Breath was walking in the cool of the Garden with Adam. That Voice or Breath had taken on a different dimension than what we think. It had shape, form and substance. It was the innocence of God so tangible it could be felt. That same Breath in Adam enabled him to be the first priest unto God, Melchizedek.

This Breath:

Set him apart from all created

Enabled him to rule over creation

Maintained his spiritual position

Sanctified and made him holy

Made him innocent and kept him innocent

The word of God always has the Breath of God, or restoration of innocence within it. Behind it, pushing with force and power to perform it. Within it, sustaining and creating it. Before it, releasing our ears and eyes   and clearing the path to receive it.

Revelation 19:8 And to her was granted that she should be arrayed in fine linen, clean and white : for the fine linen is the righteousness of saints .

White is not only the color of holiness but also the color of innocence. All innocence has holiness attached with it as well as righteousness. Holiness always has God's Breath within it. White is a color that represents joy and victory as well. Jesus as the Lamb of God is a reflection of the innocence of God.

It is one thing for Jesus to cleanse us and say we are not guilty, but it is another thing to actually walk as if we are. The problem is the reality of what we have received has not been manifested to us in a way that settles the issues.

- Innocence is not automatically restored when we realize we are forgiven.
- Innocence is not automatically restored by grace or mercy.

Innocence is restored by God doing a supernatural act that we do not fight but allow to come! There has to be acceptance on our part.

Jeremiah 15:19 Therefore thus saith the LORD, If thou return, then will I bring thee again, and thou shalt stand before me: and if thou take forth the precious from the vile, thou shalt be as my mouth: let them return unto thee; but return not thou unto them.

Being God's mouth piece is not mimicking the written word we have memorized but carrying a word that has His Breath within it. It requires holiness and righteousness. We have had righteousness restored by God's action through his Son, but holiness is restored by our actions and decision of our heart.

1 Peter 1:15-16 But as he which hath called you is holy, so be ye holy in all manner of conversation ; 16 Because it is written, Be ye holy; for I am holy .

Shame is what the enemy uses to destroy us and steal our innocence. But Jesus not only took sin away at the cross but the shame that holds us as well!

Hebrews 12:1-2 Wherefore seeing we also are compassed about with so great a cloud of witnesses, let us lay aside every weight, and the sin which doth so easily beset us , and let us run with patience the race that is set before us , 2 Looking unto Jesus the author and finisher of our faith; who for the joy that was set before him endured the cross, despising the shame, and is set down at the right hand of the throne of God .

Ezekiel 37:9 Then said he unto me, Prophesy unto the wind , prophesy, son of man, and say to the wind, Thus saith the Lord GOD; Come from the four winds, O breath, and breathe upon these slain, that they may live .

The prophetic word of these Melchisedec priests will carry such life that it will cause life to come to a dead army! You see a dead army is an army that has lost innocence. It is an army who understands righteousness but does not rise up in it. SO BREATH MUST COME. It is an army that once righteousness comes, it is repositioned and once holiness comes, it causes a different function. This is when we will know innocence is restored, when our function changes.

WHO WILL CARRY SUCH BREATH THAT HAS HOLINESS AND RIGHTEOUSNESS IN IT?

WHO WILL RELEASE INNOCENCE BACK INTO THE PEOPLE OF GOD?

John 20:22-23 And when he had said this, he breathed on them , and saith unto them, Receive ye the Holy Ghost : [23] *Whose soever sins ye remit, they are remitted unto them; and whosesoever sins ye retain, they are retained .*

This was not about them judging sin or being the final one to decide if they are forgiven. It was about treating them as restored. It was about restoring innocence by the Spirit of God. Like Peter's shadow was the radiance of holiness touching all who passed by him.

Acts 5:15 Insomuch that they brought forth the sick into the streets, and laid them on beds and couches, that at the least the shadow of Peter passing by might overshadow some of them .

Shadow means 'a shade caused by the interception of light. An image cast by an object and representing the form of that object'.

Peter was not reflecting a shadow like we think but was reflecting a holiness so deep it touched the hearts of all those around. It is the same meaning as "overshadowing" on the mount of transfiguration. Peter's shadow was healing, "the representation of the form of the object" The healing was only a representation of the object being reflected. Think how deep was the presence of God upon Peter!

Innocence releases us from presumption to a place of absolute trust. It bring us to point of having no fear and walking in faith. If we truly desire to see God in His beauty, we need to see ourselves first as innocent. Innocence is being unreserved before God. Every inhibition is gone and all that remains is total trust.

Greg Crawford

Chapter 7

Melchisedec And Gods Seven Spirits

Hebrews 7:3 Without father, without mother, without descent , having neither beginning of days, nor end of life; <u>but made like unto the Son of God</u>; abideth a priest continually .

The author of Hebrews is talking of Melchisedec. He gives some of the qualifiers. He does not have a traceable natural lineage. He is an eternal being. He states he is made like unto Christ.

Made like = to cause a model to pass off into an image or shape like it. 2 to express itself in it, to copy. 3 to produce a facsimile.   4 to be made like, render similar.

RT – a separation or breaking a union with something in fellowship with **<u>The origin of the cause</u>**

RT - to be made like or carry the likeness of

When we become born again, we begin a process of identification with Christ and taking on the image of Jesus. We actually are adopted into a spiritual family and Kingdom that does not have a traceable natural lineage as it is spiritual. Along with this, we also enter into a state of becoming an eternal being.   We have already looked briefly at Adam as the first Melchisedec priest. But we can easily begin to see there were others acting in this role. Enoch was a friend of God. In the book of Enoch, he acted as a Melchisedec priest between God and man. In the book of Hebrews, Shem was called the King of Righteousness or Melchisedec. We have looked at David as well. As we turn to the New Testament, we see the early apostles moved in this Melchisedec Priesthood. Peter, James, John and Paul all took on these dynamics to the fullest extent and were able to teach from this eternal perspective. They were possessed by the Spirit of the Lord and moved not just in anointing or waiting for a set moment but moved out of the Glory of God.   This new dynamic of priest will be carriers not just of the Breath of God but also the seven fold Spirit of the Lord spoken of in *Isaiah 11*. These seven spirits will also have the seven voices of Ps 29:3-9.

The seven voices come from the seven spirits of God. In this Ps we see the voice, thunders, is powerful, full of majesty, breaks, divides, shakes, and makes or creates. These all align directly to the seven spirits of God.

Revelation 3:1 And unto the angel of the church in Sardis write; These things saith he that hath the seven Spirits of God, and the seven stars; I know thy works, that thou hast a name that thou livest, and art dead .

Revelation 4:5 And out of the throne proceeded lightnings and thunderings and voices: and there were seven lamps of fire burning before the throne, which are the seven Spirits of God .

In the Old tabernacle, they had a lamp stand with seven lights burning, this represents that the Spirit of God can be before the throne and upon man at the same time.

Revelation 5:6 And I beheld, and, lo, in the midst of the throne and of the four beasts, and in the midst of the elders, stood a Lamb as it had been slain, having seven horns and seven eyes, which are the seven Spirits of God sent forth into all the earth .

These seven spirits also relate to the seven eyes and horns of God. The horns represent authority. David was anointed with a horn not a vial like Saul. The eyes represent perception. The eyes of the Lord run to and fro… I believe horns or authority directly relates to being anointed to be a King, a righteous ruler within the Kingdom. I believe eyes represents holiness --- being a priest before the Lord and looking at the condition of all things like a watchman.

Isaiah 11:2 And the spirit of the LORD shall rest upon him, the spirit of wisdom and understanding, the spirit of counsel and might, the spirit of knowledge and of the fear of the LORD :

1.   The opening is the dictation of the King of the Kingdom

2.   The 6 remaining spirits can be categorized into 3 areas:

1. Wisdom and understanding --- spiritual government

2. Counsel and Might --- spiritual warfare

3. Knowledge and fear --- spiritual leadership

I believe over the next few years we will see the forming of this and the emphasis of each section coming into play. If God is building a house, he will set government, conquer all that opposes, and then lead!

Since the spirit is resting upon, seven times, we need to know what exactly is meant. The word Spirit means 'breath, wind, mind, to be refreshed, breath or wind in motion'.

- Breath that carries the power of life
- Breath that carries courage
- Breath that carries value
- Breath that carries activity and life
- Breath that entered Adam that was more than
- Breath that is the entire immaterial consciousness of man

This breath has innocence in it forming righteousness and holiness in its purest form. The seven Spirits of God will carry both of these – righteousness and holiness. Just as this breath comes into man and returns to God at death so do these seven Spirits of God.

Isaiah 55:11[1] So shall my word be that goeth forth out of my mouth: it shall not return unto me void, but it shall accomplish that which I please, and it shall prosper in the thing whereto I sent it.

Word means **"dabar"** speak, speech, communication,

- The word returns back to God --- it makes a complete circle
- What happens is we are put into the circular loop and put ourselves into the pathway of the word.
- It impacts us then returns back to God after it has created something.

It is this circular Breath of God we intercept like Peter's shadow, people seeing visions and lives being touched. We came into the pathway of God's spoken word or Dabar. God's words do not stop or just come and drop off but return to Him once they are done. They stay in motion in hopes we will intercept them and make them a reality for a season upon the earth. When they no longer are needed to hold that reality, they return back to the Lord. Just like our physical life returns back to God at death.!

1 Samuel 3:19 And Samuel grew, and the LORD was with him, and did let none of his words fall to the ground .

What words ?   "Dabar" - God's words! In this sentence, the word for Spirit does not mean the human spirit --- or the Holy Spirit -- but the Breath and words of God. The Spirit (Breath of God) will rest upon him!

Spirit of the Lord

Lord means Jehovah, the existing one, LORD. It comes from a root word meaning to exist or be in existence,

Yahweh – the personal name of the Lord to dictate WHO IS RESTING UPON

Rest means to settle upon and remain,

- it means the absence of movement,
- the state of well being,
- the absence of disturbance from external causes,
- Security with victory

In other words, Lordship is settled and remains in place not moving bringing well being.

- This is about the very nature of Christ formed within us!
- It is about the Existing One resting in such fashion, He remains upon us!
- It is the awareness of God so great that things do not distract us.

This is the Breath of the Existing one or that which can bring into existence !

The Spirit of Wisdom

This is a wisdom that is not human but divine. It is inspired. It is having the Mind of Christ. Wisdom is always associated with reformation. This is a wisdom that is in its purest state ---- both having righteousness and holiness.

Wisdom means 'a manner of thinking and attitude concerning life's experiences; including matters of general interest and basic morality'.

These concerns relate to prudence in secular affairs, skills in the arts, moral sensitivity, and experience in the ways of the Lord.

It is divine and moral wisdom over secular and humanistic ability attained. It is:

"The breath of divine wisdom and moral ability"

When we speak a word of wisdom, we do it under the anointing and by the Holy Spirit speaking to us. This wisdom is God Himself speaking to us by His breath to reveal His character and morality (righteousness and holiness). This is wisdom that not only discerns between good and evil but sets a course of action based upon that discernment. It requires a response of the heart and body to engage.

Proverbs 24:3-4 Through wisdom is an house builded; and by understanding it is established : 4 And by knowledge shall the chambers be filled with all precious and pleasant riches .

Builded means 'to rebuild, establish or continue'

It is a spiritual structure or pattern. It is God's sovereign righteousness reflecting in His purposes. When the term 'build' is used in scripture it is almost always associated with Yahweh. That is because it is always about what He has said and not what we have assumed or decided to copy in building. Wisdom is always connected with a deep expression of the full measure of Christ's character allowed to be expressed.

Spirit of Understanding

Understanding means 'discernment, consider, perceptions'

Like wisdom is the mind of God bringing reformation, understanding is the heart of God bringing awakening. It is knowledge beyond gathering of information or data. It is knowledge as if being an eye witness and then you act on the presentation of God's revelation given to you. It is discerning not just good from evil but good from good as well. It is setting a value system in place to always be able to choose "the best thing." It is determining the present truth needed and then to deliver it. This is not just recognizing the times and seasons but also discerning what to do with the time and season.

Spirit of Counsel

Counsel means 'to advise, advisement, to give counsel and purpose'.

It is a counsel that is kingly in nature and priestly in focus. It can mean to devise a plan and strategy and bring hidden insights to light. It is a counsel that is eternal in nature and expects eternal results if what is said is heeded. This eternal counsel of the Lord determines what will remain forever as the Breath of God will create it!

Spirit of Might

Might means 'strength, power, bravery, A royal power'

This is not physical strength or endurance but is supernatural ability to do feats beyond human reasoning. Having might was celebrated in the Old Testament. Samson was a man of might. Gideon was a man of might. It is having the ability to see the outcome before going into battle. It is having such an assurance of who God is that no matter what the circumstance, God can perform what He said.   It is being fearless in endeavors and almost reckless in faith. It is staring at situations but the situation does not lead to discouragement but only lends itself to encourage.

Spirit of Knowledge

Knowledge = cunningness, skill

Unlike the other "Spirits of the Lord", this one is not always divine.

- This is a knowledge of intellect
- This is a knowledge of personal and technical ability

- This is knowledge of moral compass (tree of good and evil)
- To be possessed by God

Isaiah 11:9 They shall not hurt nor destroy in all my holy mountain: for the earth shall be full of the knowledge of the LORD, as the waters cover the sea .

Habakkuk 2:14 For the earth shall be filled with the knowledge of the glory of the LORD, as the waters cover the sea .

Spirit of Fear of the Lord

Fear = fear, terror, fearing. 1A fear, terror. 1B awesome or terrifying thing (object causing fear). 1C fear (of God), respect, reverence,

There are five types of fear in the Bible:

- This is not a fear in the mind- intellectual fear of evil
- This is not an emotional fear
- This is not righteous behavior leading to piety
- This is not worship done in fear of the unknown

- This is a reverential fear --- a positive fear --- always associated with God Himself.

The fear of the Lord is to hate evil (Prov. *8:13*), is a fountain of life (*14:27*), it tendeth to life (*19:23*), and prolongeth days   (*10:27*). Numerous passages relate this fear of God to piety and righteous living: it motivates faithful living (*Jer. 32:40*). Fear of God results in caring for strangers (*Gen. 20 ; 11*). Just rule is rule in the fear of God (*II Sam. 23:3*). Fear of the Almighty does not withhold kindness from friends (*Job 6:14*). Economic abuses against fellow Jews were contrary to the fear of God (*Neh. 5:9*). The fear of the Lord turns men from evil (*Prov. 16:6*).

The enabling presence of the Lord that keeps us in reverence to not be disobedient.

The fear of God so grips us because we realize who He is that we only want His heart!

Voice with the Spirit

As God's Spirit or Breath comes upon, so does its expression go out!

Psalm 29 holds seven distinct voices:

Psalm 29 [1] *Give unto the LORD, O ye mighty , give unto the LORD glory and strength .* [2] *Give unto the LORD the glory due unto his name; worship the LORD in the beauty of holiness .* [3] *The voice of the LORD is upon the waters: the God of glory thundereth: the LORD is upon many waters .* [4] *The voice of the LORD is powerful ; the voice of the LORD is full of majesty .* [5] *The voice of the LORD breaketh the cedars; yea, the LORD breaketh the cedars of Lebanon .* [6] *He maketh them also to skip like a calf; Lebanon and Sirion like a young unicorn .* [7] *The voice of the LORD divideth the flames of fire .* [8] *The voice of the LORD shaketh the wilderness; the LORD shaketh the wilderness of Kadesh .* [9] *The voice of the LORD maketh the hinds to calve , and discovereth the forests: and in his temple doth every one speak of his glory .* [10] *The LORD sitteth upon the flood; yea, the LORD sitteth King for ever .* [11] *The LORD will give strength unto his people; the LORD will bless his people with peace .*

Majesty full of = honor, excellence, splendor
       Spirit of the Lord

Maketh hinds to calve = create
    Spirit of wisdom

Breaketh cedars = break down, break out, shatter or destroy   Spirit of understanding

Shaketh earth = form or bring forth
    Spirit of Counsel

Powerful = strength, might
        Spirit of might

Divides flame of fire = to hew from or dig
            Spirit of knowledge

Thundereth = to cause to tremble
    Spirit of fear

The outcome is four things:

1.   Everyone speaks of His glory
2.   The Lord sits up the Throne as eternal King
3.   The Lord gives strength to His people
4.   The Lord blesses His people

Chapter 8

7 Fold Spirit Functions Through 7 Graces

Revelation 1:4–5 (KJV 1900) — 4 John to the seven churches which are in Asia: Grace be unto you, and peace, from him which is, and which was, and which is to come; and <u>from the seven Spirits which are before his throne</u>; 5 And from Jesus Christ, who is the faithful witness, and the first begotten of the dead, and the prince of the kings of the earth. Unto him that loved us, and washed us from our sins in his own blood,

Revelation 3:1 (KJV 1900) — 1 And unto the angel of the church in Sardis write; These things saith he <u>that hath</u> the seven Spirits of God, and the seven stars; I know thy works, that thou hast a name that thou livest, and art dead.

I love how everything in heaven evolves and is in motion around the Throne. The Throne is the stationary place of authority, non-changing and everlasting. The seven spirits we see here are before the Throne. The word "before" means to be present in His sight. It comes from two words meaning in a fixed position to be seen. "Spirit" in the shortest definition means breath. So it actually can mean there are seven breaths of God in a fixed position being constantly seen and looked upon by God upon the throne! Now that's exciting since we have been talking about the breath of God for over two years and who is carrying breath and who is not. *Rev. 3:1* shows these breaths can be possessed and refers to Jesus possessing these. So as Jesus possessed these breaths, the eye of the Father was upon Him! He was peering down and seeing how Jesus would steward these breaths. What would go into motion? Who would be touched? Now that is really deep. We call them the seven fold anointing of Christ found in *Isaiah 11:1-3*. But in reality, they are not truly anointings, nor are they gifting. Anointings are to meet a specific need present and are not dependent upon the state of the person moving under that anointing. Anyone can be anointed even an ass. The same is true with gifting. Giftings are divided to several as the Spirit wills. All can prophesy and move in the gifts of the Spirit. So to look at the seven spirits of *Isaiah 11:1* and say they are anointing or gifting diminishes the dynamic of what these seven breaths really mean.

When the breath of God comes, it has the ability to create changes. This is not a onetime event but sets something in motion of ongoing change. In other words, these seven spirits or breaths are actually seven graces of Christ (the already anointed One) the Messiah (gift given) carried. It was not the fullness of an anointing or divine enablement, even though that was always present, but was an actual grace. This is not a saving grace which most of us equate grace with. It is an ability to bring a shift where needed, confront what is needed and set the course for a fresh new thing. As Jesus, Paul, Peter, Timothy and others moved in these breaths and set things in motion, the eye of the Father was upon them as well.

Anyone can be anointed. Anyone can have a gift flow through them. Both are generally towards individuals. What I am talking about is a grace that is for the corporate Body! Paul said in *Eph 3:1* that he had been given a dispensation of grace or a stewardship of grace. If he is talking about salvation grace, then Paul would be determining who would be saved. Paul was talking about how he released and stewarded the graces upon his life. Grace is the expression of your relationship with God. Actually grace is also the pathway of how holiness is expressed to others. Holiness is not expressed through gifts or anointings. When holiness is sustained in lives, then we begin to see the fullness of grace or one of the seven fold breaths of God begin to be truly established. The deepest relationship is a relationship of holiness, — - the foundation, the essence of God, by holiness —

85

the function of God's seven graces, <u>in holiness</u> — the state of existence created by the seven graces.

Isaiah 11:1–3 (KJV 1900) — 1 And there shall come forth a rod out of the stem of Jesse, And a Branch shall grow out of his roots: 2 And the spirit of the Lord shall rest upon him, The spirit of wisdom and understanding, The spirit of counsel and might, The spirit of knowledge and of the fear of the Lord; 3 And shall make him of quick understanding in the fear of the Lord: And he shall not judge after the sight of his eyes, Neither reprove after the hearing of his ears:

Most of the Church is in the first breath or the place of 'the Spirit of the Lord is upon me'. This breath or grace is the place of salvation and deliverance. It is the place the gifts of the Spirit begin to flow. What is happening in this grace is the Lordship of Christ is being developed in an individual. This is the place the realities of what we call Biblical world view principles are formed. There are four principles that set the course for our belief system that all things flow from. Knowing God as creator, He is Lord of that creation, He is sovereign and He is providential. This is a grace that shifts us into a true understanding that we are eternal beings with eternal purposes to be exercised by our lives. Without this first grace developed, we will lack community and connectedness with a Body of believers. We will break covenant with those we walk with. We will abandon the promises given us and settle for typical Christian lifestyle. We will not have assets to be used by God. But if we truly embrace this breath to come into our lives, it will touch every hidden corner just like the wind to get into every crevasse of our heart. This grace settles identity. This is the place we see ourselves as a gift to others and that God has anointed us to be that gift. It settles not just who we are but what our primary assignments are. This grace gives us access not just for forgiveness, the beginning stages, but to be holy, the finished stages. It is a grace that gives us the greatest advantage. It is a partnership that is covenantal with the Lord and others. When Jesus stood in *Luke 4:18* and declared the spirit of the Lord was upon Him, He stated that God had consumed Him in this breath and grace. He knew His assignment. He knew His purpose. His identity was settled. Eternity was bearing down upon Him. He and the Lord (Jehovah, the all existing One) were in a total partnership. He was His representative upon the earth. This first grace and the last, the fear of the Lord are key to unlocking the remaining. Without Alpha and Omega, we will never see the others

Seven Fold Spirit or Graces

We will continue on the seven graces that Christ ministered fully in. We will now jump to the last one as without it we will never be able to move in the other five graces fully. The fear of the Lord is the other bookend that holds the rest of the graces in place. With the true Spirit of the Lord on one end and the spirit of the fear of the Lord on the other end, we end up with an open ended belief system. We also end up with graces trying to move in our lives but not being truly effective because the boundaries are not n place, thus God cannot allow these graces to fully flow.

Isaiah 11:1–3 (KJV 1900) — 1 And there shall come forth a rod out of the stem of Jesse, And a Branch shall grow out of his roots: 2 And the spirit of the Lord shall rest upon him, The spirit of wisdom and understanding, The spirit of counsel and might, The spirit of knowledge and of the fear of the Lord; 3 And shall make him of quick understanding in the fear of the Lord: And he shall not judge after the sight of his eyes, Neither reprove after the hearing of his ears:

The verse above also says God wants to bring a quick understanding of this grace. For God to add that in the description and focus upon only this one, it holds a great importance and key. The fear of the Lord is not terror or dread. Nor is it even an emotional response of surprise, etc. It is a holy reverence for God because of the awesomeness of seeing Him for who He truly is. This ability to see comes from the depth of relationship of allowing or recognizing the Spirit of the Lord is upon me. The awe of God allows us to see who we really are and what we have been redeemed from. It brings great humility with it as well. A servant's heart is formed by having the fear of the Lord and without this, the other five graces will not really operate. This is the place from which obedience comes. Not obedience by forced actions to be accepted or to feel approval, but because of heart condition and reverence. The fear of the Lord is His delight says *Isaiah 3:3.* God does not delight in our terror of Him but rather our respect of Him. It is what brings heartfelt repentance and ongoing heart examination to see if our condition is right. Without the fear of the Lord, people will live a mixed life and allow worldly things to be part of their makeup. We see much of this in Christian life as we have lost our reverence and awe of God. Proverbs also says this "Fear "will lead us to wisdom. It is not human wisdom Proverbs is talking about but the grace of wisdom, the seven fold breath of wisdom.

This "breath of awe" comes down upon us and as it does so, it brings a portion of heaven with it. It is like a portal placed upon our heart to treasure the eternal realm and thus we safeguard it. Without this in place, we will never truly cherish the other graces as they come upon us. This second breath is the breath now coming upon the Church. It is the breath that causes decisions and long term commitments to the assignments. It causes a resolve in current and future covenants. It causes a great strength to come forth upon those who breathe this breath in and allow it to come upon them. It also shifts us away from having a natural fear of rejection, men's opinions, and failure. It brings a convincing of complete victory and overcoming obstacles because of the awe of knowing the One who sits upon the Throne. This shift allows the other graces to move freely and have their full effect as they bear down upon humanity. Faith is release through the other graces in full potential and impact. The fear of the Lord is also an element that needs to be in place as it causes great faith to arise for the future and the assignments of the Lord.

There have been times the presence of the Lord has visited me and great awe was upon me as I literally hid from God. Isaiah had this experience in **Isaiah 6** as he sees himself as undone and a man of unclean lips. He saw that unless God determined he had come to the true point of reverence for Him that he could not carry the breath God wanted to give him. The spirit of the fear of the Lord would release the other graces for Isaiah, specifically, wisdom, understanding and might. God pronounced him clean and in that pronouncement, he received the breath of those graces!

We also see Paul in his encounter on the Damascus road being confronted and having Godly fear. The outcome is God heals Paul's physical eyes, which is a type and shadow of his spiritual sight. Paul steps into the eyes of his understanding being enlightened.

Ephesians 1:17–23 (KJV 1900) — That the God of our Lord Jesus Christ, the Father of glory, may give unto you the spirit of wisdom and revelation in the knowledge of him: 18 The eyes of your understanding being enlightened; that ye may know what is the hope of his calling, and what the riches of the glory of his inheritance in the saints, 19 And what is the exceeding greatness of his power to us-ward who believe, according to the working of his mighty power, 20 Which he wrought in Christ, when he raised him from the dead, and set him at his own right hand in the heavenly places, 21 Far above all principality, and power,

*and might, and dominion, and every name that is
named, not only in this world, but also in that
which is to come: 22 And hath put all things under
his feet, and gave him to be the head over all things
to the church, 23 Which is his body, the fulness of
him that filleth all in all.*

This again is not natural understanding but the
spirit of understanding, the breath of
understanding. Paul knew instantly the time and
season of God and stepped into the functioning of
those graces needed. I believe each person has
certain graces assigned to them at birth to be
engaged with through life. It is God's plan of
success for us.

The Spirit of Wisdom and Understanding

Continuing on with the seven graces found in
Isaiah 11:1-3, we now turn to what is between the
book ends of the breath of God, and the breath of
the awe of the Lord. We look at the spirit or breath
of wisdom. This is life experience to a degree but
only a small degree. The word 'wisdom' here
actually means a skill for war and advancement. It
is a word associated with spiritual battles and
mobilization of others for conflicts to move the
Kingdom forward. It is almost like what we call an
art form, of knowing how to bring people into their

destiny.

The spirit of wisdom is seen in how we act out our lives before others. It is the reflection of our heart and what we truly believe. It is the place that we make choices and decisions. We either believe God is victorious and can gain victory in all things or our lives will reflect the areas we don't believe God has this power. It is also the place confidence comes from for the implementation of promises and prophetic words God has given us. We generally describe this grace this way as life experience gained to be shared with others. In reality, that is what is produced after this grace has been allowed to function in a person's life for a season.

Natural wisdom or intellectualism is the furthest thing from the breath of God that comes from the Throne in wisdom. With natural wisdom, we can build anything. The tower of Babel is a good example of this as God said "Man could do anything his mind was set upon". We also see this in the development of society, medicine, science, etc. Generally today we think people have wisdom when they have built large ministries but a good administrator can do that. How many large ministries are making a skillful advance of bringing the Kingdom of God into the earth to change the course of societies and cultures? Yet this is what

Jesus did. This is what Paul and many others did.

This grace is the grace to receive the large plan of God. It is the rally call to come around and implement. Most are not willing to submit themselves to this nor do they desire it. The lack of instruction from the source of change is hurting the advancement of the Kingdom. Without this breath being allowed to function, the Body becomes disjointed. People abandon their post and lose heart in what God has promised.

The spirit of wisdom is also the place revelation comes from in a way. It is the connectedness revelation needs to be most efficient. It is the reason revelation comes and is needed. It is needed by teachers and other fivefold ministry gifts as they must not only know the times and seasons (spirit of knowledge) but what to do in that season (spirit of wisdom) to effectively equip the saints. It is the plan of God to be implemented upon the earth that all others things must revolve.

The spirit of understanding is different that the spirit of wisdom. As the spirit of wisdom is the plan of advancement, the spirit of understanding means to perceive and to discern by the Spirit. It is the place of rightly dividing the Word of truth and the intentions and motives that people display. It is the knowing in the Spirit that goes beyond what you see with your natural eyes and hear with your natural ears. It is the place that true covenants are made between people, vision for others and their gifting is put in place and real community is formed with purpose. The breath of understanding is also required to lead gatherings into fullness. It is the fusing together of a people to be one heart and mind containing one passion and desire. It is the motive behind the instruction of the saints. It is to be protected and moves to hold true doctrine in place, and moves in discipline and correction when necessary. If a person lacks in any of these, then the spirit of understanding is lacking. It was breathed out at Pentecost as they, as a community, had discernment and covenantal purpose. It was what launched the early Church to be fully dynamic. Without all these parameters in place, the other breaths or graces have only a small impact. Most people right now have the Spirit of the Lord, are coming into the spirit of fear of the Lord and a handful of forerunners are in the Spirit of Understanding. You see this grace requires you to stand where others will not stand. You must remain standing when others abandon and to eventually pull others up into the place you're standing so you can move on to other assignments.

The spirit of understanding is one of the greatest

advantages as it multiples the other six giftings. It even deepens the Spirit of the Lord and the spirit of the fear of the Lord. It brings great perception to the other graces. It allows the other graces to connect to purpose and motive. It keeps hearts in check before the Lord. It reveals wrong purposes and agendas as well. Without the spirit of understanding, wrong or mixed doctrine is birthed. Functions are lacking and people are not developed in their gift and calling. Overall, the Body is fragmented.

This breath and grace of God requires us to go deeper, to the point where deep calls unto deep (extreme to extreme). This is the place we truly know the intentions of the Father and we become partners in safeguarding His heart.

But this grace has an ability to connect joint to joint. What most people do not understand in all these graces is when they "move on" from a Body functioning in these, they are abandoning the grace upon that group. Thus like Paul said, they frustrate the grace and make it of no effect. This is why some receive from a group or Body because of the grace they stepped into. They then try to find grace in other groups and it might not be active or even be released. A person should find the grace upon a group and then engage in that grace even if it requires them to leave soul ties and structures carrying no life to a structure that has life.

The Spirit of Counsel, Might and Knowledge

This time we look again to *Isaiah 11:1-3* and look at the Spirit of Counsel, Spirit of Might and the Spirit of Knowledge. The spirit or grace or breath of counsel is beyond human understanding or reason. The word 'counsel' means purpose, devised advice. It is a counsel that comes only from being in God's presence. It is a counsel you can receive through others, but only, once again, if they truly have been in God's presence. This is a counsel that is not so much seeking the advice for our own lives, is seeking the advice to know what would please God's heart. It is the place that prayer is formed and from it, is activated. It is the place team ministry is formed as teams come before the Lord to seek His counsel concerning doctrinal issues, direction, and the sending forth of ministries. We see examples of these in *Acts 13* and *15.* This counsel eventually creates a oneness that Jesus spoke of in *John 17.* The union with Christ that concerns His perfection, His Word, the Son, and His glory. This grace enables leaders to make wise decisions concerning their future because it is the future that God has determined and not ourselves. This is also the place that we receive our promises that God has given us and where those promises are birthed. This counsel goes beyond the counseling of someone through their problems or issues of life, but is a special grace counsel that enables a person to step forward into their destiny and fulfill the call of God upon their life.

The spirit of might is beyond our human strength and abilities. The word 'might' means a force, bravery, mighty acts and deeds. It is the place the spirit of God is released through the working and manifestation of great signs and wonders. It is where boldness comes from that enables us to go forth and proclaim and demonstrate the Kingdom of God. There is a special grace that is beyond us moving in just an anointing or an enablement of the Spirit. This is the place where the Spirit of the Lord leads us not just on an adventure that has no meaning, but on a manifestation and demonstration of the Kingdom. This is where we go forward in confident faith overcoming all obstacles in opposition and facing those things which we have never faced before in our life. It is the place where we make decrees. It is the place where we confront principalities and powers and demonic forces. It even gives us the enablement to face martyrdom in situations that put our life in peril. It is also the place of greatest reward and seeing God move in the greatest ways. Throughout history there have been men that were graced with this special grace and nature of God. The spirit of might comes to vessels that have died to self and selfish ambitions. The spirit of might also comes to those who have no concern for worldly gain or the affections and accolades that people would bring them. The spirit of might is a special grace that causes the activation of the creativity of God and sees the breath of God be manifest in the Earth. It brings results when results can be brought no other way.

The spirit of knowledge is not intellect, or intellectual assent, or human reasoning but goes beyond how we even define the word 'knowledge'. Knowledge means the cunning ability to know the intentions. It means to know the times and seasons of God and what to do in those moments. Not only is it the nature of God but it is also a special grace that enables a person to hold fast to the promises they have received until they are fully manifest. By knowing the times and seasons, a person does not have discouragement as they know that all things said will surely come to pass. It is also the ability to discern between spirits and what is clean and unclean. It is to know the real intentions behind a person's motive and actions. This grace has the ability to rightly divide the Word of God as well. You cannot have the spirit of knowledge without the fear of the Lord because without godly fear, knowledge puffs up. Without the fear of the Lord, knowledge will kill the life flow of God as a person eats from the tree of knowledge and not the tree of life. This spirit of knowledge is the tree of life. The spirit of knowledge of knowing the intentions and times and seasons has an effect on all of the others for spirits of the Lord.

The seven spirits of the Lord or graces are the only true graces that will remain when all things have failed. The seven graces are what the Lord is endeavoring to do in building community amongst His people. The seven spirits of the Lord or seven graces are also the seven natures of God. They are not only descriptive but also reveal function as well. These seven graces allow our limitations to be removed once we are close with them. Jesus wore the seven graces as a garment as a coat of many colors that was woven by the hand of God into His very life and existence. The woman with the issue of blood that reached out and touched the hem of His garment was actually touching the undergarment of Jesus as it hung down. The undergarment was a garment that was woven out of one single-strand and was what was covering in the hidden place. These graces are coming upon the Church or in the hidden place that not many see. But they are forming a single garment or mantle that we are to be wearing, the very nature of the

Lord. As we begin to wear these breaths of God as part of our life, it will be attractive to those that are in need and they will reach out toward us to have that touch that can heal and set them free. Let us endeavor not just to seek after the gifts of the Spirit but to begin to pursue the seven spirits, the seven breaths, and the seven graces of the Lord.

Greg Crawford

Chapter 9

Melchisedec and the Four Anointings

Psalm 110

¹ The LORD said unto my Lord, Sit thou at my right hand, until I make thine enemies thy footstool . ² The LORD shall send the rod of thy strength out of Zion: rule thou in the midst of thine enemies . ³ Thy people shall be willing in the day of thy power, in the beauties of holiness from the womb of the morning: thou hast the dew of thy youth . ⁴ The LORD hath sworn, and will not repent, Thou art a priest for ever after the order of Melchizedek .

⁵ The Lord at thy right hand shall strike through kings in the day of his wrath . ⁶ He shall judge among the heathen, he shall fill the places with the dead bodies; he shall wound the heads over many countries . ⁷ He shall drink of the brook in the way: therefore shall he lift up the head .

Vs. 1-3 Apostle --- Governmental Ruling

Vs. 3, 4-5 Priest--- Throne room encounters

Vs. 6 Prophet --- God's Justice coming to earth

Vs. 7 King--- Kingly position and function

Anointing in Iowa   Melchizedek Priesthood

Daniel - Apostle   Sees the Kingdom in the
future   Spokesmen of God   Release mysteries

Enoch-   Priest   Saw the Kingdom as it is
      Friend of God   Birthed what is eternal

Isaiah-   Prophet Sees the Kingdom from the
beginning   Mouth piece of God   Releases
finishing anointing

Joseph-   King   Saw the Kingdom now   Those
who know refuge   Releases
Generations

The Melchisedec Apostolic Function

Daniel -   Apostle"Seeing the Kingdom in the
      future"   "Spokesmen of God"   "Release
      mysteries"

Psalm 110:1-2

*[1] The LORD said unto my Lord, Sit thou at my
right hand, until I make thine enemies thy
footstool . [2] The LORD shall send the rod of thy
strength out of Zion: rule thou in the midst of thine
enemies.*

Sending is an apostolic word --- sending the "rod of
thy strength"

      This was a commissioning

Rod = the staff, the rod, the branch, company led
by chief with staff

- It is about the stretching forth over a city or land
- It is about God's hand being extended

When we led the procession around the Masonic temple, we led with a staff.

Rod of strength

Strength =ocurrences; AV translates as "strength" 60 times, "strong" 17 times, "power" 11 times, "might" twice, **"boldness"** once, "loud" once, and **"mighty"** once. **1** might, strength. 1A material or physical. 1B **personal or social or political.**

In the Greek, it means = **a condition in which one can exert great force or withstand great force, with a focus of having ability to do what is desired, intended, or necessary**

The name of the hurricane approaching us is *Gustav,* and right now all of the Gulf Coast from the Florida Panhandle to Texas is on alert. The experts say that the most likely area of landfall lies between Houston, Texas and Mobile, Alabama.

The meaning of the name *Gustav* is "royal staff," "staff of the gods" or "God's staff", depending upon which dictionary definition is used.

Moses took the staff (NATURE OF GOD) and with it in his hand, loosed God's hand!

Melchisedec priests are about to rise with the hand of God so upon them

Like Moses extending his hand so when they extend theirs, a great force will be loosed.

Zion

This rule is coming forth from Zion ==== "the parched Place"

Isaiah 2:2-3

[2] *And it shall come to pass in the last days, that the mountain of the LORD'S house shall be established in the top of the mountains, and shall be exalted above the hills; and all nations shall flow unto it.* [3] *And many people shall go and say, Come ye, and let us go up to the mountain of the LORD, to the house of the God of Jacob; and he will teach us of his ways, and we will walk in his paths: for out of Zion shall go forth the law, and the word of the LORD from Jerusalem .*

To build the house, the establishment of the ROD OF HIS STRENGTH must be in place

The law and the word shall both come from ZION

Law = prophetic instruction or priestly instruction

Word = DABAR – that which carries God's breath, speak, speech, communication,

- The word returns back to God --- it makes a complete circle
- What happens is we are put into the circular loop and put ourselves into the pathway of the word.
- It impacts us then returns back to God after it has created something.
  - "I sent my word and it healed them"

Law-His rule His justice *Prophets and Priest*

Enoch-   Priest   Saw the Kingdom as it is
Friends of God   Birthed what is eternal

Isaiah -   Prophet   Sees the Kingdom from
beginning   Mouth piece of God   Releases
finishing anointing

Word- his heart   through Apostles and Kings

Joseph-   King   "Saw the Kingdom now"
"Those who know refuge"   "Releases Generation"

Psalm 110:2

[2] The LORD shall send the rod of thy strength out of Zion: rule thou in the midst of thine enemies .

Rule = translates as "rule" 13 times, "dominion" nine times, "take" twice, "prevaileth" once, "reign" once, and "ruler" once. **1** to rule, have dominion, dominate, tread down. 1A (Qal) to have dominion, rule, subjugate. 1B (Hiphil) to cause to dominate.

> Greek - **rule over**, dominate, direct, lead, control, subdue, i.e., manage or govern an entity, people or government with considerable or forceful authority

Vs. 3 thy people shall be willing ----- translates " thy people will be free will offerings"

Enemies =hostile personally and hostile nationally

> Enemies are created by victories over them
>
> Enemies are a sign of God's sovereignty
>
> Enemies are a sign of having God's favor

Proverbs 16:7

[7] When a man's ways please the LORD, he maketh even his enemies to be at peace with him.

This is the apostolic dimension that is now being birthed

The Melchisedec Priestly Function

Enoch- Priest   Saw Kingdom as it is   Friend of God   Birthed what is eternal

Psalm 110:3-5

[3] *Thy people shall be <u>willing</u> in the day of thy <u>power</u>, in the beauties of holiness from the womb of the morning: thou hast the dew of thy youth . [4] The LORD hath sworn, and will not repent, Thou art a priest for ever after the order of Melchizedek . [5] The Lord at thy right hand shall strike through kings in the day of his wrath .*

<u>willing</u> = voluntary or free- will offering

- Costing no money
- Not being enslaved
- Extravagant giving to point of excessive and too much
- Having no guilt

Now we see why God restored innocence last week ----

<u>Power</u> = strength, might, efficiency, wealth, army. 1A strength. 1B ability

RT – to whirl about or dance or shake

It means to birth forth in the pain of labor and to dance or whirl in a circle

<u>Only priests can enter the beauty realm and describe the beauty at the throne.</u>

<u>Anything we describe about the throne is not imagery or actual substance but it is all holy! Holiness in its purest form!</u>

<u>Holiness is now becoming attractive to the next generation.</u>

<u>Holiness will become fully attractive as Melchisedec priests enter the throne room and minister to the Lord and return and minister to God's people.</u>

The Melchisedec prophetic ministry

Isaiah -   Prophet   Sees the Kingdom from beginning   Mouth piece of God   Releases finishing anointing

Psalm 110:6

[6] He shall judge among the heathen, he shall fill the places with the dead bodies; he shall wound the heads over many countries.

- **Judging is judicial action occurring before the throne**
- **This is the prophetic revealing of the hearts of the unsaved to see their need of salvation**

- Also putting in motion prayer against the enemies of God
- Wounding heads of many countries is about principality warfare

This is prophecy again as in Rev.

Revelation 10:8-11 And the voice which I heard from heaven spake unto me again, and said, Go and take the little book which is open in the hand of the angel which standeth upon the sea and upon the earth . ⁹ And I went unto the angel, and said unto him, Give me the little book. And he said unto me, Take it, and eat it up; and it shall make thy belly bitter, but it shall be in thy mouth sweet as honey. ¹⁰ And I took the little book out of the angel's hand, and ate it up; and it was in my mouth sweet as honey: and as soon as I had eaten it, my belly was bitter . ¹¹ And he said unto me, Thou must prophesy again before many peoples, and nations, and tongues, and kings.

again = a new, further, in repletion of an action, the marker of adding to an existing idea

Rt word = wrestling (a contest between two in which each endeavours to throw the other, and which is decided when the victor is able to hold his opponent down with his hand upon his neck

Prophesying to --- peoples, nations, tongues and kings

Melchisedec prophets will enter the throne and eat of book set aside for them!

It is a little book meaning the assignment is very precise and pinpointed.

What God wants prophets to consume will not be easy to take or desired but when it is released, it will carry sweetness with it.

It has had time to be digested and when released the breath of God will carry it forth.

The Melchisedec Kingly Ministry

Joseph- King   Saw the Kingdom now
Those who know refuge   Releases Generations

Psalm 110:7

> *7 He shall <u>drink</u> of the brook in the <u>way</u>: therefore shall he lift up the <u>head</u>.*

Elijah drank in the brook until it dried up.

David drank in the brook.

Drink = a banquet, "Eating, drinking, and rejoicing" is used with variations to describe the feasting associated with celebrations

HE – Jesus

The brook is in the way ----- the way of the Lord not the human pathway.

<u>Way</u> = the course of life and moral character

> The Kings' highway --- Is. 35   highway of holiness

It is the same way as Is. 2:2-3

> > What will occur as we "teach us his ways"

<u>Head</u> = first" six times, "principal" five times, "rulers" twice, and translated miscellaneously 23 times. 1 head, top, summit, upper part, chief, total, sum, height, front, beginning. 1A head (of man, animals). 1B top, tip (of mountain). 1C height (of stars). 1D **chief, head (of man, city, nation, place, family, priest). 1E head, front, beginning. 1F chief, choicest, best. 1G head, division, company, band. 1H sum.**

The King will take pleasure in and even banquet with his people!

Luke 24:28-34 And they drew nigh unto the village, whither they went: and he made as though he would have gone further . 29 But they constrained him, saying, Abide with us: for it is toward evening, and the day is far spent. And he went in to tarry with them . 30 And it came to pass, as he sat at meat with them, he took bread, and blessed it , and brake, and gave to them . 31 And their eyes were opened, and they knew him; and he vanished out of their sight . 32 And they said one to another, Did not our heart burn within us, while he talked with us by the way, and while he opened to us the scriptures ? [33] And they rose up the same hour, and returned to Jerusalem, and found the eleven gathered together, and them that were with them, [34] Saying, The Lord is risen indeed, and hath appeared to Simon.

The Lord spoke to me and this is what He said:

He will ignite a new fire in many hearts just like these two. For others it will add a new flame that when added will begin to even engulf the current fire within. In either case, this will cause many doubts and unbelief to be swallowed up in fiery passion. It will not be something coming upon us but rising within us. If we allow it to rise, we will be changed into ones to influence others with the encounter we had with the Lord.

He said what He will do is challenge our hearts to open before Him, just like these two in the scripture. It will be optional for us to decide because He will make it plainly visible before us. Once the decision is made, the fire will catch. The burning these two experienced was only the embers being touched by the breath of God as Jesus spoke. It was not so much the words spoken as it was the breath released. Once the words came, the revelation was caught and the fire took hold dictating actions. It was because the Spirit and the Word both were forming and moving. The Spirit formed the fire and the Word moved the fire! When Jesus broke the bread, he was acting as a Melchizedek priest! His words and actions had the breath behind them, releasing and creating the intentions of God into these two men's lives. The encounter came from within not from without. Their hearts connected with the heart of God! They saw like He saw, heard His words and moved by His presence within their hearts. This brought a greater motivation and even a need to tell others! They carried something back to the other disciples! When they arrived and started to speak of the moment that shifted all things, the moment the High Priest released what would get beyond the impasse, literally the very Presence of Jesus entered the room to the apostles. They moved from having an encounter to carrying the presence and even the breath of God that would remove doubt and release faith.

This priesthood we are looking at far exceeds what has been. If we are not careful we will settle for an Old Testament priesthood understanding.

Heb. 7:15-16   "it is a better priesthood than Aaron's"

In Aaron's priesthood, the high priest had a special turban with a crown on it that was written "Holiness unto the Lord". It was worn when Israel dedicated to the Lord things that were connected with iniquity. This is a priesthood of not living to be like Jesus but Jesus living through us. That was the original intention of God.

It is a priesthood that not only carries the nature of God but the very breath of God as well. "Ruwach", pronounced "roo'akh" is the word for "Breath". There is 1 1/2 pages of definition for this word. A very short definition would be "wind, by resemblance of breath; a sensible or violent exhalation; life; the wind is regarded in Scripture as a fitting emblem of the mighty penetrating power of the invisible God".

Quote from 1679 prophecy to the Sons of God -- Charles Price

"*Some trials will be absolute necessity for clearing away the remaining infirmity of the natural mind and burning of all wood, nothing shall remain in the fire, for as the refiner's fire, so shall he purify the sons of the kingdom.*"

"*Some will be fully redeemed, being clothed upon with a priestly garment after Melchisedec order, qualifying them for governing authority; for it is required on their part to suffer the fanning of the fiery breath, searching every part within them until they arrive at a fix body from whence the wonders is to flow. Upon this body will be the fixation of the Urim and Thumim that are the portion of the Melchisedec priesthood, whose genealogy*" *is not counted in the creation which is under the fall, but in another genealogy which is the new creation.*

These priests will have a deep inward search and divine sights into secret things of deity. They will be able to prophesy on clear grounds, not darkly or enigmatically, for they will know what is couched in the first originality of all beings, in the eternal antitype of nature, and will be able to bring them forth according to divine counsel and ordination. The Lord sweareth in truth and righteousness that from Abraham's seed after the spirit, there shall arise a holy seed which shall be manifested in the last age."

Hebrews 5:1-2

[1] For every high priest taken from among men is ordained for men in things pertaining to God, that he may offer both gifts and sacrifices for sins : [2] Who can have compassion on the ignorant, and on them that are out of the way; for that he himself also is compassed with infirmity .

Hebrews 5:5-6

[5] So also Christ glorified not himself to be made an high priest; but he that said unto him, Thou art my Son, to day have I begotten thee . [6] As he saith also in another place, Thou art a priest for ever after the order of Melchisedec .

Hebrews 5:7-11

[7] Who in the days of his flesh, when he had offered up prayers and supplications with strong

crying and tears unto him that was able to save him from death, and was heard in that he feared; [8] *Though he were a Son, yet learned he obedience by the things which he suffered;* [9] *And being made perfect, he became the author of eternal salvation unto all them that obey him;* [10] *Called of God an high priest after the order of Melchisedec.* [11] *Of whom we have many things to say, and hard to be uttered, seeing ye are dull of hearing.*

The priesthood of Aaron   Priesthood of Melchisedec

 Taken from men   Begotten by God
(Fathered by God naturally & spiritually)
                                Same as Paul begot Timothy

Ordained for men   Ordained for God

Offered sacrifices for sin   Was the sacrifice for sin

Had compassion because of infirmity   Suffered because of love

God distinguishes which priesthood He belonged to

Vs. 5   Order of Melchisedec

Order = an arranging, arrangement. **2** order. **2A** a fixed succession observing a fixed time. **3** due or right order, orderly condition. **4** the post, rank, or position which one holds in civic or other affairs. 4A since this position generally depends on one's talents, experience, resources. 4A1 character, fashion, quality, style.

Suffered = 1 a : to submit to or be forced to endure ⟨*suffer* martyrdom⟩

   b : to feel keenly : labor under   ⟨*suffer* thirst⟩

   2 : UNDERGO, EXPERIENCE

   3 : to put up with especially as inevitable or unavoidable

   4 : to allow especially by reason of indifference

   This is knowing your actions will produce suffering not suffering that comes unaware because of your actions!

Hebrews 7:1-3

   ¹ For this Melchisedec, king of Salem, priest of the most high God, who met Abraham returning from the slaughter of the kings, and blessed him ; ² To whom also Abraham gave a tenth part of all; first being by interpretation King of righteousness, and after that also King of Salem, which is, King of peace ; ³ Without father, without mother, without descent , having neither beginning of days, nor end of *life; but made <u>like unto</u> the Son of God; abideth a priest continually .*

- The phrase "without descent" is translated from the Greek *agenealogetos*.
- DESCENT = NOT OF THE HUMAN RACE, WITHOUT A TRACED GENEALOGY,
- This **word does not mean the absence of ancestors, but the absence of a traced genealogy**.
- To the Jews, a traceable genealogy was of utmost importance, especially for the priesthood.
- If one could not prove his lineage he was barred from being a priest (Nehemiah 7:64).
- There is no recorded genealogy of Melchisedec**. His descent was not important because his priesthood was not dependant on it.**
- His lineage did not affect his right to the priesthood.

The Aaronic priests could not begin to serve as a priest until they were twenty-five years old, and had to retire when they reached the age of fifty (Numbers 4:1-3, 22-23, 35, 43; 8:24-25). Age was very important to the Aaronic priesthood, but not to Melchisedec's.

Hebrews 7:3 says Melchisedec was "made like unto the Son of God; abideth a priest continually."

LIKE UNTO = to cause a model to pass off into an image or shape like it. 2 to express itself in it, to copy

Even in the OT, Shem the king of Salem was a model of Christ but did not know Christ!

It does not say that Melchisedec was the Son of God pre-incarnate, but rather he was like the Son of God.

- being someone and being like someone are two entirely different things.
- If Melchisedec was not a man, then we have two beings who share the Melchisedecian priesthood, both being like the other, but not the same person.

The Melchisedec Priests arising will so take on the nature of Christ they will Resemble JESUS!

Greg Crawford

Greg Crawford

Chapter 10

Melchisedec Functions

Revelation 1:1-3

[1] The Revelation of Jesus Christ, which God gave unto him, to shew unto his servants things which must shortly come to pass; and he sent and signified it by his angel unto his servant John : [2] Who bare record of the word of God, and of the testimony of Jesus Christ, and of all things that he saw .

[3] Blessed is he that readeth, and they that hear the words of this prophecy, and keep those things which are written therein: for the time is at hand .

Reading the book alone does not bring revelation.

John did three things

> Bore record of the Word of God

> Bore record of Jesus' Testimony

> Bore record of all things he saw

So we are required to "readeth and hear" and "keep those things written".

The book is about more than Jesus, but is about the REVELATION OF Jesus Christ. It is about what He received that He was able to give to John or reveal to John. It is about the quickening of our eyes and ears to perceive the same Revelation that Jesus HAD!!!

Rev. 1:1 The Revelation of Christ was given to Jesus to show His servants.

Servant = a bond slave, a love slave, **one who gives himself up to another's will, those whose service is used by Christ in extending and advancing His cause among men. 1C devoted to another to the disregard of one's own interests.**

- **This type of servant is more than a disciple but a reformer**
- **Mysteries are for reformers**
- **This revealing of Christ's mystery is the true empowering of Christ within us.**

It is more than a disciple but takes the position of a reformer.

Revelation comes to reform more than to disciple.

Discipleship is Christ in us.
Reformation is Christ through us.

Discipleship is us abiding in Christ!
Reformation is Christ abiding in us!

A disciple of Christ is one who

(1) Believes His doctrine

(2) Rests on His sacrifice

(3) Embraces His Spirit

(4) Imitates His example

Luke 14:26 If any man come to me, and hate not his father, and mother, and wife, and children, and brethren, and sisters, yea, and his own life also, he cannot be my disciple.

Luke 14:27   And whosoever doth not bear his cross, and come after me, cannot be my disciple.

Luke 14:33 So likewise, whosoever he be of you that forsaketh not all that he hath, he cannot be my disciple.

Discipling is to be an act of pastoring. It requires disciplines. We have made pastoring to be pacifying. We don't expect a pastor to help us grow but to appease us. If disciples were formed in the church, reformers would be turned out of Bible Schools. But consequently most bible schools work on putting foundations in place making disciples by the time they graduate.

Hebrews 9:10 Which stood only in meats and drinks, and divers washings, and carnal ordinances , imposed on them until the time of reformation .

- These things only affected the outward man and if not careful our discipling will only allow outward change.
- **Reformation must occur within us before reformation flows out of us**

<u>Time</u> = Kairos of reformation

<u>Reformation</u> = setting in order, sitting upright, to cause to stand erect,

> to erect settlements, cities and governments

<u>It actually means a setting in order because a set time has occurred dictating it!</u>

<u>This order has several areas to it.</u>

- Melchisedec order----- the functional position of the final age Priesthood
  - Five fold fully mature and functioning
  - Ecclesia fully functional
  - True disciples operating in priesthood of believers
  - Five spiritual senses energized
  - Revelatory encounters and third heaven ministry to the Lord
  - Stewarding second heaven
  - Ministry into the earth
  - Revealing of God's heart to us, mysteries revealed

- Kairos order ---- the eternal synergy of the final age
  - Fullness of all things being revealed
  - The eternal flow of the spirit – the expansion of divine moments
    - Revealed in how we do gatherings
    - Revealed in revelatory preaching
    - Revealed in prophetic ministry outside church settings

- o The pressing in of the next age into this one
  - ▪ Eschatology (study of end times) will be addressed and shifted
  - ▪ Eternal mindsets will dictate temporal pleasure
- o The cry of creation for the sons of God fulfilled
  - ▪ Creation itself will partner with the sons of God
  - ▪ Creation will easily bow to commands that have God's breath

- • Manifestation of the sons of God order -- the revealing of the greatest mystery of the Kingdom age, the heart of God toward His creation. The breath of God manifest
  - o The illumination of light and truth
  - o The lifting of veils from minds
  - o The redemption of humanity and the earth
  - o The creative breath of God flowing
  - o The transcending and transformation of the earth, society and culture
  - o Mysteries manifest
  - o When these sons find fatherhood, the Church will find assignment

Revelation 1:1-3

[1] The Revelation of Jesus Christ, which God gave unto him, to shew unto his servants things which must shortly come to pass; and he sent and signified it by his angel unto his servant John : [2] Who bare record of the word of God, and of the testimony of Jesus Christ, and of all things that he saw .

[3] Blessed is he that readeth, and they that hear the words of this prophecy, and keep those things which are written therein: for the time is at hand .

Jesus' Revelation was given to John to understand by His breath

Seven spirits holding the seven breaths of God

From = a separation of motion from an origin point

Notice he says these breaths are before the throne and   come from Jesus.

Revelation 1:4-6 John to the seven churches which are in Asia: Grace be unto you, and peace, from him which is, and which was, and which is to come; and from the seven Spirits which are before his throne ; [5] And from Jesus Christ, who is the faithful witness, and the first begotten of the dead, and the prince of the kings of the earth. Unto him that loved us, and washed us from our sins in his own

131

blood , [6] And hath made us kings and priests unto God and his Father; to him be glory and dominion for ever and ever. Amen .

> Vs. 6 John receives from Jesus the order of Melchisedec

> Vs. 6 John receives and sees the extension of the Kairos into a continuous moment

> Vs. 6 John sees the outcome of dominion that will occur through the sons of God

2 Timothy 3:16[6] All scripture is given by inspiration of God, and is profitable for doctrine, for reproof, for correction, for instruction in righteousness:

<u>Correction</u> = reformation

One expectation Paul had towards Timothy as a son was the ability to reform by addressing issues.

- But notice these not only come by just teaching the scriptures
- <u>These come by inspiration = God Breathed --- ruwach</u>
- <u>Reformers do these things listed, not disciples</u>

<u>The first order of reformers is to awaken other reformers</u>

Colossians 1:25-27 Whereof I am made a minister, according to the dispensation of God which is

given to me for you, to fulfil the word of God; [26]
*Even the mystery which hath been hid from ages
and from generations, but now is made manifest to
his saints:* [27] *To whom God would make known
what is the riches of the glory of this mystery
among the Gentiles; which is Christ in you, the
hope of glory*:

- It is the progressive unfolding revelation
  that He is giving us and it was for the
  saints of the day
- This mystery is more than Christ in us, it
  is given to FULFILL THE WORD OF
  GOD!
- It is the abiding of Him that shows us the
  things that must shortly come to pass

Because Paul was not just in Christ but Christ was
abiding in him, he was able to see the same
mystery that Christ saw concerning the end of the
age saints. Paul was hoping the Colossians would
experience this same understanding.

**Christ abiding in us is the only way to unlock end
time events in this age.**

Paul probably felt the manifestation of the sons of God would be his generation. Some of the saints comprehended what he was talking about referring to the "mystery" but the majority did not comprehend.

Galatians 1:16 To reveal his Son in me, that I might preach him among the heathen; immediately I conferred not with flesh and blood:

Galatians 2:20 I am crucified with Christ: nevertheless I live; yet not I, but Christ liveth in me: and the life which I now live in the flesh I live by the faith of the Son of God, who loved me, and gave himself for me .

Galatians 4:19 My little children, of whom I travail in birth again until Christ be formed in you,

Paul never succeeded in praying this into existence. They were struggling to allow Christ to have access. Their relationship was through legalism rather than a relationship through Christ.

But a generation will come into this truth and mystery to make a way for "Christ to appear" (not rapture) in the world.

2 Corinthians 4:7 But we have this treasure in earthen vessels, that the excellency of the power may be of God, and not of us.

1 Timothy 1:16 Howbeit for this cause I obtained mercy, that in me first Jesus Christ might shew forth all longsuffering, for a pattern to them which should hereafter believe on him to life everlasting.

Ephesians 3:16-17 That he would grant you, according to the riches of his glory, to be strengthened with might by his Spirit in the inner man ; [17] That Christ may dwell in your hearts by faith; that ye, being rooted and grounded in love ,

Romans 8:9 But ye are not in the flesh, but in the Spirit, if so be that the Spirit of God dwell in you. Now if any man have not the Spirit of Christ, he is none of his.

John 15:1-6 I am the true vine, and my Father is the husbandman . [2] Every branch in me that beareth not fruit he taketh away: and every branch that beareth fruit, he purgeth it, that it may bring forth more fruit . [3] Now ye are clean through the word which I have spoken unto you . [4] Abide in me, and I in you. As the branch cannot bear fruit of itself, except it abide in the vine; no more can ye, except ye abide in me . [5] I am the vine, ye are the branches: He that abideth in me, and I in him, the same bringeth forth much fruit: for without me ye can do nothing . [6] If a man abide not in me, he is cast forth as a branch, and is withered; and men gather them, and cast them into the fire, and they are burned.

Vs. 2 The branches that are "in me" may or may not produce fruit

Vs. 5 Those who allow Christ "to Abide" bring forth MUCH fruit

Vs. 6   Those without Christ produce no fruit

Rom 8:19 All creation knows a great mystery will unfold at the end of the age. The ultimate result of the Melchisedec priesthood is to be the manifest sons of God that the whole earth is groaning for. The groaning is the knowledge creation has of its full redemption as well. Creation will be redeemed by these manifest sons as the very breath they speak with will be the creative force to recreate the earth into a newness, thus redeeming it. What do they look like?

They carry the very breath of God deep within their spirit. They access the heart of God and the throne room to receive instruction. They are able to bring the fathers heart into the earth in such a way men's hearts almost fail them. They speak with authority that is not just an anointing but has the breath of God within it putting things in motion to create what is needed. They prophesy from the inner most being, releasing a flow of living waters . They cause demons to tremble and principalities to give way. As manifest sons they redeem Gods creation, and will finalize the face of Christianity upon the earth. They will be the ones who will bring the kingdom of heaven into the earth in such a way that the kingdom will be fully felt by all of humanity. They are reformers and they are ones who awaken hearts into destiny and purpose of life. They release revelation and cherish the spirits presence. They waste no words pacifying emotions, but speak the truth in love so all can grow into maturity. They are misunderstood, but fully accepted by heaven. Ones the Father can rely on, working through and investing in, the mysteries of Christ. They will be the ones who present the kingdom of God to the Father and Son.

They will be ones who will pay any price and go anywhere. They will give their lives for the sake of the King and His kingdom and will choose hardship over popularity. They will cause stirring in hearts and cities and will shape and form a new face of Christianity which was the true face it was to have. They know what part of old is relevant for today and what part of truth is not the pressing point. They will release divine moments in God and atmospheres for people to access God. As priests before God and men they will hold a most peculiar position and receive a most sought after reward, the presence of the Lord. They will be common men and women doing a most uncommon thing, made fun of yet many will desire to be and live like them. You can be one of this manifest son or daughters!

Chapter 11

1679 Prophecy To The Sons Of God

Dr. Charles S. Price

A precious document found among the private papers of Charles S. Price after his passing:

Sixty Propositions: Otherwise known [in an edited modernized form] as the "1679 Prophecy". This is the source material from which many versions of the prophecy were taken. It was originally excerpted from the *Message to the Philadelphian Society*, by the followers of **Jane Lead** and published in 1697. Jane Lead's writings (including the 1679 Prophecy) and an introduction.

1679 Prophecy to the Sons of God

"There shall be a total and full redemption by Christ. This is a hidden mystery not to be understood without the revelation of the Holy Spirit. The Holy Spirit is at hand to reveal the same unto all holy seekers and loving enquirers. The completion of such a redemption is withheld and abstracted by the seals of Revelation. Wherefore as the Spirit of God shall open seal after seal, so shall this redemption come to be revealed, both particularly and universally. In the gradual opening of the mystery of redemption in Christ doth consist the unsearchable wisdom of God which may continually reveal new and fresh things to the worthy seeker. In order to which the Ark of the Testimony in Heaven shall be opened before the end of this age, and the living testimony herein contained shall be unsealed.

"The presence of the Divine Ark (Christ) will constitute the life of this Virgin Church, and wherever this body is, there must the Ark of necessity be. The unsealing of the living testimony within the Ark of God must begin the promulgation of the everlasting gospel of the Kingdom. The proclamation of the testimony will be as the sounding of a trumpet of alarm to the nations of professed Christendom. Authority shall be given by Christ to the putting an end to all controversies concerning the true church that is born of the New Jerusalem mother. This decision will be the actual sealing of the body of Christ with the name (or authority) of God, giving them a commission to act by the same. This new name (or authority) will distinguish them from the seven thousand names of Babylon.

"The election and preparation of this Virgin Church is to be after a secret and hidden manner. As David in his ministry was chosen and anointed by the prophet of the Lord, yet was not admitted to the outward profession of the kingdom for a considerable time afterward, of the stem of David a Virgin Church, which hath known nothing of a man or human constitution, is to be born, and it will require some time for it to get out of the minority and arrive at full and mature age.

"The birth of this Virgin Church was typified by St. John's vision where the great wonder appeared in heaven, bringing forth her first born, that was caught up to the throne of God (or identified with the authority of God). For as a virgin woman brought forth Christ after the flesh, so shall a Virgin Church bring forth the first born after the Spirit, who shall be endowed with the seven spirits of God. This church so brought forth and sealed with the mark of divine authority will have no bonds or impositions; but the holy unction among these new born spirits will be all in all.

"There is not at this day (1679) visible upon the earth such a church; all profession being found light when weighed in the balances. Therefore they are rejected by the Supreme Judge, which rejection will be for this cause, that out of them may come a new and glorious church. Then shall the glory of God and the Lamb so rest upon this typical tabernacle, so that it shall be called the Tabernacle of Wisdom, and though it is not now known in visibility, yet it shall be seen as coming out of the wilderness within a short time. Then will it go on to multiply and propagate itself universally, not only to the number of the first born (144,000) but also to the remnant of the seed, against whom the dragon will make war continually.

"Wherefore the spirit of David shall revive in this church and most especially in some elect members of it as the blossoming root. These will have might given them to overcome the dragon and his angels even as David overcame Goliath and the Philistine army. This will be the standing up of the great prince Michael, and it will be as the appearing of Moses against Pharaoh in order that the chosen seed may be brought out of hard servitude.

"Egypt doth figure this servile creation under which Abraham's seed groans, but a prophet, and the most prophetical generation, will the Most High raise up who shall deliver His people by the force of spiritual arms; for which there must be raised up certain head powers to bear the first office, who are to be persons in favour with God whose dread and fear shall fall on all nations visible and invisible, because of the mighty acting power of the Holy Spirit which shall rest upon them. For Christ will appear in some chosen vessels to bring into the Promised Land the New Creation state.

"Thus Moses, Joshua, and Aaron may be considered types of some upon whom the same Spirit will come, yet in greater proportion. Whereby they shall make way for the ransomed of the Lord to return to Mt. Zion; but none shall stand under God but those who have become "tried" stones after the pattern and similitude of Christ. This will be fiery trial through which a very few will be able to pass or bear up in it. Whereby the waiters for this visible breaking forth are strictly charged to hold fast, and wait together in the unity of Pure Love. This trial will be of absolute necessity to all for the clearing away of all remaining infirmities of the natural mind, and the burning of all wood, hay, and stubble. For nothing must remain in the fire, for as a refiner shall He purify the sons of the Kingdom.

"There will be some who will be fully redeemed, being clothed upon with a priestly garment after the Melchisedec order. This will qualify them for governing Authority. Therefore it is required on their part to suffer the Spirit of burning and fanning of the fiery breath searching every part within them until they arrive at a Fixed Body from whence the wonders are to flow out.

"Upon this body will be the fixation of the Urim and Thummim that are the portion of the Melchisedec priesthood whose descent is not counted in the genealogy of that creation which is under the fall, but in another genealogy which is a New Creation. Hence these priests will have a deep inward search and divine sight into secret things of Deity; will be able to prophesy in a clear ground; not darkly and enigmatically, for they will know what is couched in the first originality of all beings, in the eternal anti-type of nature, and will be able to bring them forth according to the divine counsel and ordination.

"The Lord sweareth in truth and righteousness that from Abraham's line, according to the Spirit, there shall arise a holy seed, produced and manifested in the last age. The mighty spirit of Cyrus is appointed to lay the foundation of this Third Temple and support it in building.

"There are characteristics and marks whereby the pure Virgin Church shall be known and distinguished from all others that are low, false, and counterfeit. There must be a manifestation of the Spirit whereby to edify and raise up this church, bringing heaven down upon the earth and representing here the New Jerusalem state, in order to which spirits are thus begotten and born of God, ascended to New Jerusalem above where their Head in majesty doth reign.

"None but those who have so ascended and received His glory can condescend and communicate the same, being thereby His representatives upon the earth and subordinate priests under Him now. He that has ascended and glorified has made Himself, as it were, our Debtor. Consequently, He will not be wanting in qualifying and furnishing certain high and principal instruments who shall be most humble and as little regarded as David was, whom He will dignify with honour and priestly sovereignty for drawing to them the scattered flocks, and gathering them into one fold out of all nations.

"Therefore, there should be a holy emulation and ambition stirred up among the bands of believers that they may be of the first-fruits unto Him that is risen from the dead, and so be made principal agents for Him and with Him, that they may be, if possible, of the number of the First-born of the New Jerusalem mother. All true waiters of His Kingdom in Spirit, under whatsoever profession they may be, ought to be numbered among the virgin spirits to whom this message appertains. Be watchful and quicken your pace.

Greg Crawford

Chapter 11

The Breath of God

The first breath of creation

Genesis 1:1-2 In the beginning God created the heaven and the earth . ² And the earth was without form, and void; and darkness was upon the face of the deep. And the Spirit of God moved upon the face of the waters .

This was a deliberate act of the Spirit waiting until God said ---- His breath released!

The Breath of Humanity

Genesis 2:7 And the LORD God formed man of the dust of the ground, and breathed into his nostrils the breath of life; and man became a living soul .

Breathed was an action. Breath is what was released.

The word first breath means "breath" for "blast" and "inspiration," while the former one replaces "breath" with "life.")

This noun, when used in reference to man, generally signifies the breath of life. It is frequently found in combination with *rûaḥ* "spirit" and seems synonymous with *nepeš* (q.v.). In KJV it is twice translated "spirit"

When God first breathed into mankind, it was more than making his lungs work correctly. The word 'breath' used here with Adam is different than the word 'breath' used in other places. Breath here means not only the essence of life or source of life, b**ut means you cannot hold or contain the dynamics of this breath unless you first have the attributes to sustain this breath.**

It is not the physical breath but the spiritual breath. The spiritual breath is creative. It holds the attributes.

The breath to understand the Eternal realm

Rev. 4 The throne has the breath of God permeating it!

Rev 4:5 There are multiple voices

Voices require breath to produce sound.

We are in heaven not the earth's atmosphere.

Literally everything John hears has God's breath through it. His breath manifests into what John sees.

Rev 4:8, 11 The highest form of worship is the worship that has God's breath through it.

John sees the heavenly realm – the throne. It also sees the very breath of God surrounding God. But John has to breathe in the breath of God to expel the breath to create on earth.

Ezekiel saw the throne and came back trying to say what he saw but it did not create like John was able to do. Ezekiel said it was like unto, and had the appearance of. Could he have not breathed in what was in the heavenly realm?

John also saw what Paul saw.

Revelation 5:9-10 And they sung a new song, saying, Thou art worthy to take the book, and to open the seals thereof: for thou wast slain, and hast redeemed us to God by thy blood out of every kindred, and tongue, and people, and nation; [10] And hast made us unto our God kings and priests: and we shall reign on the earth.

Paul explains the dimension from which this will manifest. It will be a breath for all nations.

Acts 17:24-28 God that made the world and all things therein, seeing that he is Lord of heaven and earth, dwelleth not in temples made with hands ; [25] Neither is worshipped with men's hands, as though he needed any thing, <u>seeing he giveth to all life, and breath,</u> and all things ; [26] And hath made of one blood all nations of men for to dwell on all the face of the earth, and hath determined the times before appointed, and the bounds of their habitation ; [27] That they should seek the Lord, if haply they might feel after him, and find him, though he be not far from every one of us : [28] For in him we live, and move, and have our being; as certain also of your own poets have said, For we are also his offspring .

Breath ---- néō, empnéō.

1. *pnéō* denotes a. the blowing of the wind, b. breathing or snorting, c. wafting forth, and d. full of, or panting for.

2. The first two senses occur in the LXX (cf. the wind in **Ps. 148:8** and the breath of God in **Is. 40:24**). *empnéō* occurs for the inbreathing of the soul in **Gen. 2:7.**

3. In the NT the blowing of various winds is what is meant in **Mt. 7:25 ; Jn. 6:18 ; Lk. 12:55 ; Rev. 7:1** . The blowing of the wind denotes the Spirit's work in **John 3:8** . Only in **Acts 9:1** do we have the sense "breathing out" (*empnéō*).

4. The sense "to be fragrant" occurs in Mart. Pol. 15.2 (the scent of the dying martyr is like incense) and Ignatius *Ephesians* 17.1 (the anointed Jesus wafts incorruption on the church as a divine fragrance).

God decided to SHOW His breath and its manifestation!

Acts 2:1-2 And when the day of Pentecost was fully come, they were all with one accord in one place . [2] And suddenly there came a sound from heaven as of a rushing mighty wind, and it filled all the house where they were sitting.

one accord – homathumona --- having the same passions

There "came" = to come into existence, to begin to be, to appear in history,

What is really happening at penitcost is the breath of God is released because of the passion and zeal of men being unfied in passion. That type of passion allowed something never before seen to be birthed or appear in history! Now that is carrying the breath, releasing the breath, and seeing the breath create!

Sound = echoes, has two definitions

1. a report, information, blast of a trumpet
2. roar of a noise

The sound started in heaven before it was heard in earth. The sound was carried by the breath of God. It was the crossing over of sounds coming into sight. Sounds is on the same frequency as colors. When Adam and Eve heard the voice of God waking in the cool of the garden (Gen 2:8) they were hearing the breath of God. It had shifted from the invisible realm to the visible. The voice was beginning to echo in history for the first time upon the earth!

Wind = the breath of God.

Rushing = bring forth, carry, to endure or bear

Mighty = violate force

Not only did the breath create but had the ability to sustain what it created. This is a principle that the things of God are indeed eternal and will not pass away. Not only does it endure but it also becomes a force that is put in motion and stays in motion. God is not going to destroy the earth because of the principle of his breath but the breath will bring it into a new earth!

The spiritual breath has authority projected from it. Like Ezekiel saw it had the ability to raise what was dead and bring new life. It had the ability to raise an army and this is what Pentecost is about the raising of Gods Kingdom army on the earth.

Ezekiel 37:9 Then said he unto me, Prophesy unto the wind , prophesy, son of man, and say to the wind, Thus saith the Lord GOD; Come from the four winds, O breath, and breathe upon these slain, that they may live .

This breath has the ability to finish the age, and to bring things into existence new and fresh. Rev 10:11 says we will prophesy again. The word again means "A New" This is not repeating old patterns but that which has the breath of God in it. It requires not our breath prophesying but God's breath through us!

This is what John heard in Rev 10:4 with the seven thunders, seven voices. He was hearing a day the breath would be released with force and power again. We are now coming to that place and we can see people who are carrying the breath. We are coming to:

Rev. 10:6   Time (Chronos) is no longer

Rev. 10: 7   The seventh angel is about to sound.

Rev. 10:9   <u>The book he is to take and eat has been formed by the very breath of God.</u>

He is told to prophesy again (a new, further, to wrestle until you are victorious, the expansion of an already present idea) before:

>Peoples

>Nations

>Tongues

>Kings

John is told to declare prophetic truth. Truth has the breath of God. Knowledge has the breath of man. John is told he must prophesy to those (**Rev. 5**) chosen for redemption and chosen for king/priest roles.

Rev. 11:15 The seventh angel sounds and says:

Revelation 11:15 And the seventh angel sounded; and there were great voices in heaven, saying, The kingdoms of this world are become the kingdoms of our Lord, and of his Christ; and he shall reign for ever and ever.

This is the direct result of John prophesying anew or with the Breath of God. The Breath is in us if the Word is in us. The Word of God in us is the Breath of God formed into what is palatable for us to consume in our humanity. The Breath breathed by the Spirit into us, is the future of the Word about to be created out of us, consumed by the Spirit within us!

ABOUT THE AUTHOR

Greg Crawford has been active in ministry for over 30 years serving in almost every type of leadership role. He is the founder of Jubilee International Ministries which recently relocated to Des Moines, Iowa. He and his wife, Julie, have also co-labored in founding Jubilee School of Ministry and Jubilee International School of Ministry which now has 40+ schools in developing nations. The International School network graduates roughly 5,000 students yearly. They have grown the network of schools to stand on their own within their nation without ongoing support from the United States. Jubilee School of Ministry in the USA has international graduates who have established schools and works in many nations of the world as well. Many have planted churches orphanages, and are involved in high places of influence in governments. Today Jubilee School of Ministry is no longer a class room but is an online school of ministry training with over 350 hours of online instruction.

Apostle Crawford or APG as he is know by, has traveled on numerous international trips, leading teams into nations conducting leadership conferences. He has worked in Cote D Vire,

Nigeria, South Africa, Zambia, and Indonesia. Many of the nations have had reoccurring trips as he has taken teams of ministers with him. He laid the ground work for the apostolic reformation in Nigeria with close to 12 trips to this nation alone, teaching thousands of leaders on team ministry and the apostolic for the first time. With close to 50 ministers ordained under them in the United States, they also provide counsel and insight, helping many church leaders today.

Apostle Crawford has become a spiritual father to many and has a desire to see the generations running together as one voice. He has labored to see the Kingdom expression of reformation and awakening come by travels in Iowa and the United States to help bring this into existence. He is best known for his revelatory teaching style and has a unique and powerful ministry of laying on of hands for impartation. He carries a deep message that release the breath of God to confront the hearts of believers. This has opened the door for him to speak at many national conferences. The revelatory dynamic has enabled him to write over 10 books, write close to 300 hours of classes, some taught by secular colleges, and to send out a bi-monthly teaching through email. His teachings can be found on many websites and have been the lead feature article on Identity Network a leading prophetic voice in America with a web base following of close to 350,000.

He holds a PHD of Ministry which he received Magna Suma Cum Laude. He is ordained with Jim Hodges' Federation of Ministries and Churches International and is in relationship with several well know national voices. Currently he is overseeing The BASE, a ministry located in Des Moines to bring awakening and reformation to the church and culture. The forerunner ministry of the BASE has creative spontaneous worship created in the moment, gift and call devolvement, investment by spiritual fathering, and revelatory instruction with opportunity. More information can be found at the ministry website **www.thebaseiowa.org**

Greg Crawford